COBWEBS, CABBAGE AND CANNABIS

Phyllis M. Jones

Published by the Author

Published by
Phyllis M. Jones
Pen y Bont, Heol Sylen
Pontyberem, Carmarthenshire, SA15 5NW
Telephone: (01269) 870263
Fax: (01269) 870149

ISBN 0 9501891 4 6

A CIP catalogue record for this book is available from the British Library.

Printed and bound in Wales by
Dinefwr Press Ltd.
Rawlings Road, Llandybie
Carmarthenshire, SA18 3YD

Contents

Note

This book does not presume to be a reference for serious students, although the facts have been gleaned from some who have spent their lives fathoming the mysteries in the natural world we have inherited.

MISS BERYL HARDING
VALLEY VIEW, PORTSCATHO,
CORNWALL, TR2 5EB

Photographs have been provided by Miss Beryl Harding, a renowned Botanist, who has taken a life long interest in the subject.

COVER PHOTOGRAPH:

A waste piece of land in Gerrans, Portscatho, Cornwall, with help of English Nature, has been converted into a Wildlife Area, consisting of two ponds, surrounded by meadow land where many native trees are planted. This has attracted a variety of plants, water creatures and bird life.

Local schoolchildren have found this a great source of interest, visiting often to study the frogs, four species of Dragonflies and, coming especially in Spring when the Mallard Ducks have ducklings.

Introduction

This book developed as I exchanged experiences with a friend over a kitchen table.

We were of different generations but there was a similarity in the patterns of our lives. Not a rigid routine of school, social background, employment and education, not even were we from the same area. In our lives there were the same ingredients and interests. We were fascinated by the diversity of life. We liked characters who might be considered eccentric, perhaps for no other reason than they had a close association with rural life and an interest in all things living; plants which might have herbal constituents; animals and their behaviours and a willingness to take life as it came with no set convictions. This was a philosophy which we could understand and an interest to be developed.

Conversations roved over many subjects and it appeared there was a combination of mystery and ancient knowledge in all that we had taken so much for granted. I found that I had to delve into those unusual spheres more deeply.

It takes time before we notice the small monuments are obliterated by winds and weather. A pile of stones or a mound is a mark to say where there was once an old dwelling place. Some hint of how scenery has changed will be disclosed in a name. Cwm yr felin, Lletty Mawr, Cwmmawr (a large valley which is now a village) and one name which still is appropriate is that of Gwaunydd Cochion, the Red Moor, a flaming expanse in autumn composed of the mountain acres which form the top of Tumble, Carmarthenshire. Colour comes from the purple moor grass, so vivid on maturity.

Establishing a background which is uniformly Welsh was difficult because of the variety of scenery, mountains of Snowdonia; smooth contours at the edge of the sea in Ceredigion, stretches of forestry and heather in Mid Wales and long stretches of sand at Llanstephan or Kidwelly. I have concentrated on an area which has been studied by botanists because of the variety of plants, fertile soil and where the true Welsh inhabitants have farmed and mined.

We knew about the Agricultural Revolution which shook this area as much as any and caused even the London press to be aware of

Rebecca. We knew about the industrial and political changes, these are taking place around us still. A large hoarding depicting the name of a building syndicate marks a green field. Within days the hedge is demolished and turf is replaced with acres of torn earth. Within weeks lorries and other traffic, sheds and piles of building materials flow into the place and within months there is an estate which has houses crowded together with such little space between them . . . high density I think is the term to describe the new development.

So many changes and it is ironical that the development adapts a name which links the new locality to its past links.

Discovery of the route back in time means lighting fires in the hearts of people yet the interest is bound to stimulate those who are wanting to begin the study.

There is fascination and danger in research. One turns from living memories into the pages of folk history and it is almost possible to see how cottage fires were kept blazing with piles of furze. We see how wood has been stripped from large areas and how the small mines produced anthracite coal which has made the valley of Gwendraeth famous.

In fields, gorse still grows. Many bonfires started with furze from the gorse which was first planted to be used as chaff to eke out supplies of animal fodder, but when added to the baking fires it gave that extra heat to make bread and keep warm in winter. This hardy plant has played its part in the history of Wales. The standby for bonfires, used to make flames to send urgent warnings across country from mountain top to mountain top; for celebrations and for children to set shrubs alight on their way to or from school.

In peat lands tree trunks are often found and they make good hard seasoned wood for supports for houses. Forests were denuded and at first coal measures were left because the value of coal as a fuel was not realised. Iron was extracted. The Celts who must have superimposed their culture on the early inhabitants were masters of metal-work and were able to fashion cauldrons and other tools, harness and ornaments. Some were for export. Silver filigrees with coloured stones were exported as far as Babylon from 'those Barbarians beyond the sea'. In the rough peasant history however, it is enough to imagine the iron cauldrons swinging on hooks over the white hot ashes of a peat fire – swinging so as not to press the fire too tightly down to extinguish it. The fine ash kept in overnight and in the morning was blown into a new blaze, the pieces of wood not burnt were saved to give body to the first flames of the fire. Research has uncovered several similar cauldrons. These proved a link across the years with our ancestors and were to be found mostly on the farms. Some were painted and contained earth and summer flowers; others rusted and lay in outhouses along with wrecks of old cars to add to the evidence of past things. At times a small gadget would be unearthed, perhaps a pointed metal object which was used to pierce the veins of cattle for blood letting which was supposed to cure Black Fever. I saw such an object, held it in my hand . . . it was trivial really and yet something of great importance in the lives of people who farmed in the district; a length of timber honed by rain and wind was once the shaft of a wagon.

The interiors of cottages betray the ways of real rural life. Stone flags on the floor and a long slated table for salting the pig, slaughtered to feed the family during the winter. Pig meat has been a traditional food from the beginning of time. It makes one wonder about the persistent habit of having a leg of pork at Christmas. Maybe a tradition of pagan festivals. Our ancestors drank mead from the honey of wild bees, a potent drink, they ate berries, Elderberries, Whinberries, Blackberries and steeped them with their individual touches to make their wine. In winter they stored nuts which they gathered from Hazel trees which grew in abundance in the mild climate. Wheaten beer was prepared with honey. A little was drunk at the time of a feast from the cup or drinking horn when passed around, it must have been potent if one had seen the ferocity and wild antics after the feasts to celebrate battles against invaders. Vikings probably brought their own traditions. Legend tells us that for traditional feasts, food would be gathered for a year; the milk-fed hog; an ox that had been fed only on milk, grass and corn and 100 loaves baked in honey. At these feasts the hero's portion was a feature; the bravest hero coming in for the thigh bone. Wine was drunk, but the most common intoxicating drink was ale (curm Gaulish Corma). Barley was the grain most utilized in making it but rye, oats and wheat were also used. In Carmarthenshire the farms do not produce cereals successfully, however a certain amount of wheat barley and oats were grown locally. Among the varieties were Hen Gymro and Red Lammas (names that have Celtic associations. Oats Ceirch-du-bach and Ceirch-gwyn-naill-ochor, Hen Cymro. The crops were never abundant.

A place is as old as its stones. We have considered the wet earth covered by red vegetation as in Gwaunydd Cochion. We wonder about the peat in the bog lands, the wood which must have been cleared from the slopes of Cwm yr felin; the furze from gorse shrubs and the dead, red bracken. Furze and bracken when set alight gave instant heat and substantial heat when the thick part of a tall gorse shrub burnt. Underneath the mountain, stones also told a story. When miners dug further into ground than was necessary for surface mining which had been sufficient for centuries there were the fossils. Anthracite with the impress of old plants; whole tree trunks which were found in the roof of a seam in the mines. I have seen for myself a tree trunk petrified into stone, the markings on the main trunk as clear as when it grew in some ancient forest.

The Celts and presumably those other ancient Britons whose ways of life they themselves had superimposed, had ready access to salt. They were enabled to salt their meat in the autumn for preservation during the winter. Here, the long slab of slate in the preserved farm kitchen become significant. Many of us remember too how it was common for sides of bacon to hang from the rafters even until just after World War II; sometimes from the ceilings in public houses. There was milk, butter, cheese and curds and there were the root crops, turnips, potatoes and mangolds. Poaching was a gross offence and according to the law of the Commons, even the fuel, a slab of turf or 'billet' (a word still used for lumps of firewood in Cornwall.)

So much richness in the soil and surroundings and for those who would learn the secrets there were the plants with properties which could flavour and heal.

From the needs of those who once carved their lives in parts of rural Wales we have learnt and sometimes improved upon, but are beginning to appreciates.

I Just Saw the Flowers

As a child there was nothing sinful about picking flowers. They were all around us . . . in abundance. Of course, we had to be careful. Dandelions grew, even in our small patches of lawn in the front of the two up and two down houses. They were bright gold and plentiful and I could never understand why a bunch of Dandelions was a gift which brought condemnation. 'They will make you pee the bed,' my mother said, 'Don't bring them in here . . . Now mind!' This was a dire warning and I never again repeated the mistake. Outside, after they had changed to little balls of fairy feathers which we could blow and blow, like blowing out candles on a birthday cake and tell the time, we knew they did have their uses.

Groundsel could be found in small patches, maybe in the backyard or around the vegetable patch. This had to be brought in, one piece each day for our canary. He liked it and of course he had his Millet Spray.

There were other warnings. 'Never have that in the house . . . it is unlucky'. This was at the time when the hedgerows were beautiful and bunched with white May Blossom. Why were we told this when folk songs about 'Bringing in the May' were sung in schools as we held our old music books, dull green with black crotchets and quavers spoiling the impact of words. 'Never cast a clout until May is out'.

Perhaps that was it. At the time we did not connect it with the Tea Treat . . . the annual event held on May Day. This was when all the children in the town gathered in the main square and walked out into the country. This was on a special field on Treyew Road which now, I suppose, almost a century later, just counting from our parent's days, remains a focal point in the town's interest. It is a field now with tidy paths and a few seats and, although the view of Truro is framed by a wider band of housing and there is less green foliage, for us it will be unique, a focal point. So quiet, where are the children who screamed and ran and ate those large, special spiced Saffron buns (our tea treat). Only the dogs run now and older people walk or sit and watch their pets.

May Day. Afterwards children lined up in fours, the band assembled in red and scarlet uniforms which shone as the brass buttons and badges caught the lowering sun. The first Boom Boom Boom from the drums and then the blood pounding notes of the 'Floral Dance'. We danced to the beat of this music all the way back to the town. En route, everyone had to join in. The music galvanised into action all who were lining the streets, age did not seem to matter, the music was irresistible it forced us to dance. The band never stopped. There was something elemental about the tune, yet we did not appreciate sinister connotations. Not even when the Carnival Queen was seated on her decorated *(with branches of all kinds of flowers, especially white May Blossom)* was driven around the town. It was probably a farm gambo, which, drawn by a quiet horse led a myriad of dressed up characters, green men and jesters and tradesmen with their workday floats pulled by familiar ponies . . . Prince or Janey, Tommy or Maggie, their manes bright with traditional and coloured ribbons. The night would end with fireworks and a large bonfire, flames high enough to send the pagan message across the land. Each village knew the ritual, each as wild in spite of civic efforts to tame the proceedings. Padstow with its 'obby horse music and dance is equally evocative whenever I think of or hear it.

There were flowers to spare. No protection labels after their names. My sister and I spent hours once threading petals of Bluebells to make a dress so that one of us could be a princess. It was never finished. Perhaps lack of patience or a quarrel as to who would be the eventual child to wear the gown . . . maybe lack of petals.

Recent research has proved that Bluebells have a medicinal property which might be of use in a cure for cancer. This has led to yet another form of a raid in the countryside to gather in large quantities Bluebells and also a special variety of Snowdrop. I have a secret place which forms a large carpet of white in early springtime and I gloat over this vision each year.

A Lingering Crawl to School in the Early 1930s

It is so easy when one is older to repeat the words 'In my day . . .'. Yet there were innumerable differences. We walked to school. One of us called for the other and later met class mates along the way. Our routine was arranged according to the changing of seasons. There was time to watch and be aware:

> '. . . then the whimpering schoolboy
> with satchel and shining morning face
> creeps like a snail unwillingly to school.'

This quotation from *As You Like It*, sums up the situation.

The hedges were thick and green. For every plant, the hedge has existed for a hundred years it is said. Part of the way was edged by little garden walls, just right for sitting on, I do not know why our efforts could not have made us tired; perhaps a thick Privet hedge would make one garden more secluded in case there were secrets to be exchanged. There was a stretch which edged the 'Tea Treat Field', our May Day venue . . . the morning's exodus from town into the country and a reminder of the importance of May Blossom.

For the rest of the year we passed along the hedge which separated it from the pavement. A pavement which bubbled with tar during those long remembered summers. The hedge I picture in my mind. First there was the base of thick grass where Celandines and Buttercups, Sower-sabs and Yarrow, this has greyish-feathery fine-looking leaves with daisy like flowers, one of the witch-herbs to be carried at weddings, Cow Parsley and Loosestrife and the yellow Tormentil grew. Hawthorn shrubs backed this growth. Foxgloves thrust amongst them and behind, at intervals, small Oaks and Willows grew. We chewed the succulent grasses; munched our bread and cheese from the Hawthorn (the leaves), made faces as we tasted Sorrel, the Vinegar Plant as it is called back home in Wales. A leaf of Sorrel is added to my sandwich of lettuce and cheese and it does enhance the flavour.

Children from so many different areas without being taught or told seem to arrive at similar conclusions. Some plants are universal. 'The True British Herb of The Ancients' quotes Munting in Culpepper's note on Sorrel; children follow national guidance on their routines and it is mandatory to attend school; it is the blending of traditions which leads to a conclusion.

'When it springeth forth
the Cuckoo singeth most.'

On those hedgerows as we trailed to school how often did we remark on Cuckoo Spit? Goosegrass or Cleavers, Sweethearts, Clovers, Grip Grass, Robin-run-in-the-grass, Scratweed and even Mutton Chops. Most of these names are descriptive and can be understood, Sweethearts, for example, was because the little burrs clung to clothing if sweethearts had been lying in the grass perhaps in the dusk on a summer's evening. This was a sticky plant which twined with profusion amongst all the other herbs in the hedgerow. It was only after trying to trace which plant it was amongst all the names attributed to it that I realised that it belonged to the Galium Aparine (Linn) the Madder tribe. In many of the old herbals and more modern publications this plant is reckoned to be very useful. It has been used in the treatment of skin conditions, it is a powerful diuretic and because it acts so strongly on urinary secretions and urinary organs it is given as a treatment in these conditions. It even acts as a solvent when there are stones in the bladder or gall bladder. The dried plant is infused in hot water and drunk as a tea.

Culpepper, says Sorrels, are under the Dimension of Venus . . . it is prevalent in all hot diseases. It is said to cool any inflammation and heat of blood in agues, pestilential diseases or choleric or sickness or fainting arising from the heat. General information says it is useful as a laxative. But we did not know any of these things. As children we picked and chewed the delicate leaves and made faces of distaste and pleasure when the juice rested on our tongues.

Now as I learn a little more I lean towards two uses of this herb, one from *In A Wild Garden* by Roger Banks, he says he likes to take a basket, just about ten minutes before lunch and, with some children whose fingers are able to search out the most delicate of leaves, pick enough to add to the daily salad, to place in a sandwich or to put in the pot. The second idea is that Russians make a cooling drink from the infusion. Always the emphasis is on the cooling nature of the plant.

Another idea which I think would add to a summer picnic is to have a green sauce, just like the modern salsa . . . what a lovely name for a little glass dish containing a bright amount of a piquant colourful sauce. Just to add a serious thought, if the plant is beneficial to bring down a fever or even to give that comforting glow when someone is just about to go into bed with a heavy cold or influenza there is this recipe to consider . . .

A Stirrup for a Fever. 2 oz Wood Sorrel; 2 oz Lemon; crush, steep in hot water, add honey . . . hold the mug with two hands and drink.

A word of caution which seems to come through in many of the books, there is a warning that an excess will irritate the kidneys.

Meadowsweet and Woodruff gave a faint background scent and it was easy to imagine strewing these plants on the floors of the cottages or baronial halls. These were the days when Cowslips grew in certain fields and near a little boggy patch King Cups grew. Large Buttercups we thought they were . . . I suppose they belonged to the same tribe or family.

Further on there was a cultivated Bay Tree where, in response from an order from Mother, we plucked some leaves to flavour the marinating herrings in their dish of vinegar and water with salt and pepper. This, after our Bay Leaves had been added, would be covered in brown paper and allowed to cook, slowly in a night oven. On one who had experienced it could ever forget this all pervading smell.

In hot weather there was the lacy Cow Parsley; sometimes Deadly Nightshade, a sinister purple and spindly plant we knew we must never touch. I do not remember Primroses or Violets along this hedge, but little leaves of many plants were plentiful. Primroses and Violets grew in the hedgerows and fields of other walks. In real summer there would be wild roses and Honeysuckle which we would gather to place in jam jars in our homes. Henbane with its aura of evil threatens.

Years later in Wales, when I used to ride my mare around the block, I began in February to count the number of wild flowers in bloom, perhaps some Snowdrops, later there was Celandine, Dandelion, Primrose, a few berries and grass seeds; Sorrel might also be seen. In full season, Foxgloves look magnificent amongst the foliage and in some stretches the Rosebay Willow, not as unwanted weed, but in full glory. Blackberries and Gorse and the early Catkins and the Hazel would be yielding a crop of hazel nuts. Even now, when I consider these nuts

I sense a coming together of the seasons. Autumn approaches and here is a winter food amongst the green summer foliage. There will be colder months ahead and then, from bare and elegant branches of the Willow, Catkins and silky buds will announce life and the next spring.

It is September when the fruits are gathered. Country people knew how to make the most of the richness around and children in farms gathered blackberries in quantities for bottling and jam-making; whinberries when tiny fingers were an asset; mushrooms for the places where this almost magical plant grew were secrets kept for generations in some families. To go nutting was a good excuse for an outing, the phrase was evocative, it made us see the green filberts amongst the leaves and feel the tang of late summer in the air; probably it was the folk memory of rural pleasures when the world seemed much younger.

Hedgerows

Light branches bend over the Snowdrops and Daffodils, Celandines and Wood Anemones and will remind us that we have taken for ourselves Nature's forest paths. Winter ends with this gradual increase of light and faint colours, Spring has a freshness, silver and soft when growth is renewed.

Summer has such vivid colours which force moments into our minds, different times and places, with myself, are connected with Cornish Lanes or Welsh Hills.

One vivid moment was on a cycle ride to Feock as a child. I rested on a bank and I noticed the bush next to me was plastered with butterflies. In those days butterflies were never out of our lives . . . nor moths . . . at night when lamps or candles were lit they flew in through the open windows and fluttered around the light.

One story comes into my mind here, it was told by my father. 'Concerning Flanders Field. The battle which was responsible for thousands of lives and the graves that covered that field afterwards all in their straight and even rows.' He said, Poppies were growing where no flower had grown for a long time and the strange phenomenon of the red butterfly resting on these flowers and no other butterfly. Red into red into red.

Not all memories connected with plants have glamour. There is a horrible story recounted by my mother about the treatment of worms. The tape worm was mentioned. The male Fern was used and the essential oily liquid is extracted; after 24 hours fasting this is given before bedtime; castor oil is given in the morning as a purgative and infallibly the tape worm is expelled. When told with dramatic force this cure sounds drastic.

We were exploited when we were young and too foolish to realise how much. I think of the holiday . . . 'Potato Week in Wales' and as I think of schooldays when we revelled in thought of a games lesson, I shall remember the Plantain, if only because before a game of hockey or netball we had to go on to the field and dig out as many of these horrible plants as possible. Yet the Plantain is an important herb. There is also a story, which, although it happened many years after my schooldays, I think it will explain what I mean.

* * *

It was hay time on a Welsh hill-farm and the men were resting outside the barn. Tom caught his arm against a sharp piece of metal and it bled, quite a lot. Len, immediately – and they said he must have had gypsy blood in his veins – pulled up the crown of a Plantain which was growing near, he held the leaves and the spiky centre and crushed this part of the plant on to the wound. As I read now of the special healing and cleansing of this plant – Fire Weed, they called it – he did the right thing. The other men regarded him with disgust. 'Why didn't he go into the house and wash it with salt and water?' This would have been as good, but, they say that the Plantain will close a gaping wound as with a seam of gold thread, for just as gold will not admit rust, so the Plantain, will not admit rotting and gangrenous flesh.

* * *

Other varieties of leaves, picked and washed, boiled in water and crushed, are also good for poultices on badly healing wounds, sores, varicose ulcers and scabbing.

On our school walks, in shady, woody places when we were sent out on field studies, there was an abundance of 'Lords and Ladies' a plant I have not seen for years.

One household possession will be associated with winter and summer in memories of family life which I have still and treasure to the extent of being afraid to use it or move it in case it breaks. It is the roomy with glazed interior earthenware pot.

In this pot my mother made, it was said, the best Hereby Beer in Cornwall. She pickled eggs in Water glass for winter use and where she stored all those extra rich Saffron cakes made at Christmas which fed a hungry family well into the New Year. A recipe for Hereby Beer is given below:

> Pick a handful of young Stinging Nettles, Yarrow and Wild Sage, Take 2 gallons of Water, add herbs, boil all together, then add 1½ lbs. of sugar. When almost cold add 2 oz. yeast, and let it stand until the next day. Then strain through a muslin, bottle and cork. Tie down the corks firmly. It must not be drunk until at least three days old.

When gathering nettles the following advice is given (a thick pair of stockings or high boots should be worn) then with shears and a basket or 'frail' go forth. Pick them early in spring when nettles are young and tender and plentiful. However, it is possible to make this drink with young plants right through the summer. You will not be able to resist it.

My mother's Hereby Beer must have been unique. She had no exceptional knowledge of herbs. Probably she obtained the ingredients from a neighbour or bought them in a shop which specialised in herbal matters. All I know is the fermenting went on in the cool cellar under our house. Every so often there would be distress as a bottle popped its cork.

Some wines sound delicious because the name is evocative. Cowslip wine, for example, and if there had been a shipwreck in the vicinity . . . often a bottle of brandy adds to the potency.

So many recipes are available and are collected from various sources. Some will be given at the end of the book. The old fashioned remedies all seemed to have associations with warmth, comfort, candlelight and feather pillows, a shadowy figure tip-toeing from the room.

I can still smell the Camphorated Oil with our chests were rubbed when we had colds.

Note: The roasting of an onion or a potato in ashes reminds me of when I first came to Wales and I would hear tales of such feasts from the tin workers and surface workers in the mines and in the houses where there might be still those deep ash pans under the grates of anthracite fires.

Always in our kitchen cupboard there were the simple remedies of that era. I do not think it would be all that different in any other household. Later, I shall be writing more about Vick and Wintergreen which were good standbys, these were far more useful for myself in later years. But Vick was my mother's remedy I think . . . for nasal congestion, a bad chest, for bruises and strains. As I have mentioned the pungency of Camphorated Oil lingers in the mind. It was warmed after standing for a while on top of the stove. There was a different, glowing warmth when it was applied. Memory might be deceptive, but the warming glow was never unpleasant. I realise we were lucky not to have much real illness in our family.

Chemical food was a regular additive in early spring, a tonic for us after the winter; these days ample helpings of Spinach or Watercress is an acceptable alternative. If ever we were constipated there was Syrup of Figs. There were Senna Pods also in the cupboard for this purpose and Epsom Salts. Senna Pods are interesting. I read in M. J. Gieves'

Encyclopedic book that the plants are collected annually in tubs (after the rains), exposed on rocks in hot sunshine so they are absolutely dry before being stripped and packed in palm leaf bags and transported by camels to Essovan and Darao and down the Nile to Cairo. No wonder there was an exotic aura about this medicine. Later, in my hospital years, it was still in use, probably on children's wards, but it was regarded as mild, guaranteed not to cause pain through griping and even to us children who eyed any medicine bottle with suspicion, it had a nice taste. For colds the treatment was inevitable, a warm bed with a hot drink of lemon and honey. I cannot end this memory of Cornwall and my childhood without speaking of Saffron. It was a specialty, apart from cream and pasties and a seed cake made with Caraway seeds. There were never cream cakes or chocolate eclairs in our house, a confectionery shop was not used when Mother did her weekly shopping. It was even the same at Christmas, except for the rich dark Christmas cake. At this time with amazing energy, my mother made about fifteen loaves of fruity Saffron Cakes which were moist and seemed to improve with keeping. They lasted the family with all the Christmas visitors well into the new year. They were kept, of course in that lovely old earthenware bowl covered with several folds of a white sheet.

I read that Saffron is the Karcom of the Hebrews in Song of Solomon IV 14, 'Spikenard and saffron; calamus and cinnamon, with all trees of frankincense; myrrh and aloes, with all the chief spices.' The plant was known to the ancient Greeks and Romans. I report with pleasure that the European plant is rated as superior to that of the Mediterranean regions. It must have been common in England, hence the name Saffron Walden but, Cornwall is known for pasties, Saffron cakes and cream. It is expensive. Even as children when we were sent to the corner shop for an ounce of yeast and sixpennyworth of Saffron, there seemed to be only a few shreds in the triangular packet. On baking days, when I watched Mother, many times she went through the ceremonies of 'proving the yeast' with a gentle warmth and steeping the fine orange coloured shreds of Saffron in a small jug of boiling water. I have watched modern cooks on television often and have never seen them use the method.

When I came to Wales, a friend of mine, the wife of a Pharmacist, gave me her supply of Saffron which was kept in one of those drawers in a miniature cabinet. It was a gift. She said, 'No one else here will ever want it.' I use it often now with just as much ceremony when I make my special rice dishes. Thai Rice in its proportion of boiling water, made up with the juice of half a lemon, faintly flavoured with garlic and shallots, and the almost ½ teaspoonful of Saffron, once again given to me by a friend, the Saffron this time from Tunisia, makes this the most delicious of dishes. It is obtained from the Crocus and is deep orange in colour, a grain of good commercial Saffron contains the stigmas and styles of nine flowers . . . therefore, without computers, 4,320 flowers are used to produce one ounce of Saffron. It has a peculiar, aromatic scent which pervades the kitchen on baking day. The saying 'As dear as Saffron' is understandable.

It is not known exactly when Saffron was first introduced into Cornwall. It is believed the Phoenicians brought it over with them when they came to trade for tin. There are many places which are known to have been places where the Phoenicians landed their boats to trade. Indeed, there is one particular river where the legend says, Christ sailed on one of their ships when he was a boy carpenter.

Before I leave Cornwall I must give one or two recipes which prove how primitive were the lives of people at the end of the twentieth century, so often called the 'Good Old Days'; days which show a dependence on the natural world.

SAFFRON CAKE

4½ lbs flour. ¾ lb currant. ¾ lb sultanas. 1lb lard. ½ lb butter. 4 eggs. 1 oz yeast. Saffron. ½ lb lemon peel, ½ lb castor sugar. Pinch salt. Warm milk to mix.

In some recipes rose-water, seeds and spice, are added. Mostly it is a case of send it to a quick oven and an hour and a half will do it.

A recipe which won a prize in the Australian *Women's Mirror*, June 25th, 1929, sounds interesting. This is for POTATO CAKE. Take 12 medium-sized potatoes, clean and boil in skins until soft, then peel and mash while hot. Have ready in basin 1 sifted cup of flour, 1 tablespoon of butter, put mashed potatoes in with the flour and butter and half a cup of milk until an ordinary-looking pastry is made. Roll out on flour-board and put in a baking dish. With side of hand make hollows in pastry. Have ready enough bacon rashers (or, if preferred, any sliced fresh meat) to put on top of potato cake in the hollows made by hand. Bake in moderate oven until light brown. This recipe was given by Manaccan W.I.

It is true to say that although we were surrounded by most of the plants necessary to effect all the simple cures, we did not understand their value. Even those who were considered wise in these matters could not have known everything . . . the subject is so vast, there are so many small variations in the shape and colours of different plants in their own tribes. In the end there was nothing we could do against the terrible infectious diseases and illnesses which affected children. We depended mostly on care and nursing and nourishment.

In the following chapter, when I try to relate some omit experiences of my caring for animals, I feel I can understand more of those pre-antibiotic days . . . and perhaps a little of the desperation our parents felt when faced with problems which must have seemed impossible to solve.

Benefits from the Sea

Everything in my young life was enhanced by the proximity of the sea. We lived almost centrally, between the English Channel and the Atlantic, two opposite settings, with a mild English Channel and a wild Atlantic. The River Fal with its wooded banks flowed into the Channel and our leisure hours, when I was training as a nurse in the local hospital, meant the hiring of a boat and use of our waterway.

Rocks covered with Bladderwrack and this name is evocative. The plant is attached to the rocks by branched, root-like extremities which come from the underside of the stalk. The tough bladders are placed at intervals along the frond, little bubbles which we tried to pinch. It was found always on the rocks, sometimes spread with such thickness that it was a nuisance. It was easier to run across rocks when they were less covered by sea weed.

I tell stories as they enter my mind. Just at this moment I know that I cannot continue without talking about the Welsh delicacy, Laverbread. I was not ignorant about seaweed as a child, 'If you could smell seaweed you would not die of consumption,' I was told. I heard often the sad story of my mother's uncle drowning because he was entangled in the long, slippery thongs of seaweed which floated around the rocks on our Cornish shores. As children we were warned always to swim away from these areas. They were dangerous, having the trick of twining around arms or legs and making a swimmer helpless, yet as is often proved in life there is always another side and Kelp and Bladderwrack have been important in many ways. As a fertilizer it is invaluable, in Ireland for potatoes, in Cornwall for the early broccoli and everywhere, the Channel Islands depend upon it for their early Jersey potatoes which we all love. In the Hebrides the smoke is used to flavour cheese. It has been used with some success as an additive to feed horses. Some time ago when I had a gelding, Holly, which was not doing too well, I sent to Ireland for a special container of a black oozy kind of paste which was added to Holly's normal food. Seaweed was a content. He really did improve in condition in a short while. Iodine is a principle medicinal derivative. We used it for thyroid treatment in my early nursing days and also, it is an ingredient in Cod Liver Oil, a derivative mixed with grapes makes a wine, which is a good tonic for diseases of the hip, bone and joints. Apparently, it can be produced more cheaply now from other procedures, but it was very effective. The parts used are, when dried, root, stem and leaves.

It was the enthusiasm in voices as Welsh devotees spoke about Laverbread. 'It is lovely. Just dust it with oatmeal; flatten it and fry it with a bit of Welsh bacon,' they said. I saw it first in Swansea Market in a stall where they sold cockles. One of those white, clean, homely stalls where friendly faces, weathered and rosy, smiled as they passed over packets of a fish-smelling black paste. It is still sold. I last bought it in Llanelli Market, the stall maintained that clean traditional ironing-on-Monday atmosphere. I saw it last as I watched 'Ready Steady Cook' on television. Fern Britton, the programme's hostess, looked suspicious as she opened a small tin of a black paste which could have been, quite easily, Caviar.

For years a friend of mine, Meta Mayne Reid, and myself exchanged letters. Her letters were beautiful, she was a distinguished Irish writer. She described her garden, her activities, her typing of her novels in the family living-room with all its associated noise, her walks along the shores of Antrim and she spoke of Carrageen.

The name is evocative. I wish I could find Meta's letters. I never threw them away. I know they will fall out of pages of notebooks or diaries sometime in the future. She gave me a recipe. Hardly anyone, when I discussed it in those days, had heard of it – just as Laverbread was new to me once upon a time. Now, as I discussed this with Menna, my niece who is a strict Vegan, she told me she uses it as a substitute for gelatin. It is sold in the health shops.

All this emphasizes my philosophy, which is becoming more and more evident as I write, that gradually, with all our modern knowledge and technology we are catching up on the things our ancestors knew hundreds of years in the past.

Once again, I have discovered the fascination of research. In the College library I engaged the help of a colleague and we searched the internet for information on Carrageen. There was nothing to add to the bare 'edible seaweed' mentioned in Infopedia. I turned to the previously mentioned book which I keep in my kitchen cupboard and following a trail, 'Seaweed, Sea Parsley to Irish Moss and CARRAGEEN', I am able to record a few more facts. It is a moss which is found on half submerged rocks off the coasts of France and naturally off the coast of Ireland. It is noted for its mucilaginous properties and where it grows it is noted as a great help for those who suffer from tuberculosis and all the accompanying coughs and other chest problems. I quote once again, 'You won't die of consumption if you can smell seaweed.' The word mucilaginous almost explains itself, it is characterized by a gummy or gelatinous constancy which for me suggests phlegm.

The Celtic Backyard

I sat in the old kitchen at Disgwylfa. On one side of the table the settle was against the wall and ranged around the kitchen were the old tried and tested oak chairs. The ceiling was, and I say this with some regret, tobacco brown. David Jones relied on his grandchildren to bring back packets of duty-free (favourite brand) by the hundred. These days children travel further than the nearest village. Sometimes it is one good thing about a new way of life.

It was time for tea. Water had been heated by the old stove out in the lower kitchen, the pails were scalded and ready and the cows in the yard were relaxed. They knew their next move would be into the cowshed. On the table the bread and butter looked good enough for any drawing-room. The bread was fresh, the butter as good as any in the market and it was cut by David in thin even slices. He prided himself on this simple chore. No other member of the family would dare to compete.

I pulled my chair up to the nearest empty place.

Mrs Jones was pouring the tea. As I waited I looked at the bunches of dried Elderflower which were fastened along one of the beams in the ceiling. Their colour matched, almost, the ceiling. Alongside them were bunches of dried Lavender and little tied bunches of Stinging Nettles, the brittle leaves recognisable still. I had asked the old lady before, when was the Elderflower gathered. It was when the flowers were in bloom, they were brought into the kitchen to dry slowly. In winter when it was needed it was one of the most efficient remedies for colds, coughs or the 'Flu'. Mary, the daughter told me, 'A bunch would be placed in the saucepan and boiled. The liquid would be drunk when it was hot and brown sugar with a little lump of butter would be added.' She assured me, 'It never fails.'

There must be something magical about the Elderflower. Consider the old farmhouse at Disgwylfa. It is hundreds of years old. The shape of the building with thick walls and small windows will testify to that. Our house at Pen-y-Bont goes back for a few hundred years and on our deeds it says that we were part of the old Disgwylfa lands. All these years people have followed their old traditions of hanging Elder in the house. It is not only because dried Elder is a useful remedy for winter ailments, there is the fact that the Elder was always considered to be a magical tree. It kept away demons. When there were burials the undertaker or his equivalent carried pieces of elder as a protection against any evil which might threaten the dead. Ancient Egyptians had the same idea only their essentials were far more exotic. Our Celtic ancestors ensured their dead were provided with what they considered essentials. It was not wise to damage this plant on purpose and it was necessary to treat it with respect. But there were so many associations with the tree . . . cradles were never made of Elder wood; it was reputed to be the tree from which Judas Iscariot hanged himself; it was a mother figure who, among other things devoured her children. There is such a mixture of good and evil associated with the tree. I feel if it is capable of providing comfort and good to the living; it could not have been so detrimental to the dead. I have a copy of John Lust's *Herbal Book* which rests on the top of my mini-library in the kitchen cupboard. It was first published in 1974. Of course, there are many others. I refer often to Culpepper, but this is to discover how attitudes have changed or remained, towards a plant. John Lust's book is informative because of its many cross-references. It says of Elderflower that this Sambucus Canadensis, with a further identification, 'Sweet Elder' is a cathartic, diaphoretic, diuretic, purgative and stimulant. As a native plant of America, Indians used root bark tea for mucous congestion and to promote labour in childbirth. An infusion of leaves and flowers or a decoction of bark serves as an antiseptic wash for skin problems, wounds and inflammations. Flower tea, taken warm, is said to stimulate and promote sweating. This list of properties makes sense of having such a pharmacy growing so near to most of the old houses. It explains why bundles of Elder blossoms are tied and hung from the beams of farmhouse kitchens. A friend of mine explained that this was the custom in her own home and, if anyone felt a cold coming on, part of the bundle would be boiled, sweetened with honey and drunk before going to bed. Some books state that boiling must be substituted for steeping.

Elderflower is one tree which should grow within reach of everyone. It is all powerful and in spite of all the mystery with which it is associated, it is meant to do us good. The white, lacy, fragrant flowers, the heavy crop of black berries which bring wood pigeons and other bird life to add even more weight to the branches in early autumn. A man who had been a farmer asked me if it was possible for him to fill baskets and bags of flowers when, in their perfect state, would be made into wine. He suffered from emphysema, a chronic condition which has recently been rated as an industrial disease so that those affected might be due for a legal compensation. I knew him in the years before emphysema disease was given legal recognition. Alas he did not live to have any benefit through the new law, neither did his widow.

But I had heard the wheezing and rasping sounds which must have made his breathing so difficult. I almost felt the leaden heaviness in his chest. I was glad the Elderflower wine brought some relief. We gathered it when it was perfect, resting an aluminum step-ladder against the tree to pick the choicest blooms for his wife to make into wine. He gave me a bottle and I swear it has shortened many periods of influenza and colds. It eases the cough 'most powerfully'.

Our tree was never tainted by fumes from road traffic and was rated highly by the fastidious. Two friends were regular beneficiaries of our tree, they were very much up-market, their end product was Elder champagne, just as fragrant, but lighter good for social occasions. The other was an ex-miner who suffered from his chest. He believed strongly in the purity of the blossom because of his farming family background, and was assured each year of as much as he wanted from our tree.

In autumn, birds enjoy the delicacy and in spring and the sound of bird song is heard around that area. There are two Elderflower trees near our and these play a major part in the environment. At times when I see the Wood Pigeons at close quarters, I note their plumpness and when they fly from branch to branch there is so much movement that the tree seems to have a wind blowing through it, as if the tree is shaken by a gale. At the moment though there is only the fuzz around bared winter branches.

Now is the time when Stinging Nettles are young and may be used, they can be cooked almost as we cook Spinach and they can be beneficial because of the iron they contain. Lavender is at its best in July and, as this is the time of the year when flies are at their most annoying, it is as well we can use the oil from last year's plants to keep flies away in the evenings.

As I read in the reference books about Lavender, I am assured of several facts. It is a little surprising to discover that English Lavender is rated higher than Lavender grown, even in the Mediterranean and the scent, amount of essential oil present, is greater. One strange and unexpected fact recorded is that vipers, the dangerous snakes, used to inhabit the bushes of Lavender and made gathering of the plant difficult.

We all know that bunches of dried Blossom are kept between linen and the scent is delightful. Cool Lavender water in a compress placed on the forehead does soothe a headache and sweetens a sick-room, but one definite property of the plant is that Lavender will kill lice and small insects. To think that wonderful scent repels insects.

Many years ago, I can say with honesty, almost fifty, when we were playing tennis at Craig-y-nos, then a chest hospital and now a building for the production of musicals and operas, the Medical Superintendent and his wife and whoever else was playing, dabbed Lavender Oil around their faces to ward off evening attacks from gnats and other insects. The tennis courts near the river at the bottom of the grounds at Craig-y-nos were not too comfortable on those summer evenings. It was the home of Adelina Patti, the famous Italian opera singer, and when she lived there she would sometimes walk down over the lawns towards the river singing to the group of friends she had around her. Edward VII was a frequent visitor; the lady was famous and well loved in that area and entertained lavishly.

'Who'll buy my Lavender . . . sweet scented Lavender,' was the cry from the girls in Covent Garden. I wonder which songs Adelina Patti sang?

If I think of a garden devoted to herbs I think of a world of scent and living. To me, the names are evocative: Lovage and Rosemary, Thyme and Sage, Peppermint and Feverfew and Meadowsweet. The names of dangerous plants sound ominous – 'As though of Hemlock I had drunk' and Deadly Nightshade. Reading about them fascinates and confuses – there are those which are too universal in associated beneficial effects and must be true and there are those which prove the opposite. Most herbs are fascinating because they have been used in foods and as medicine for hundreds of years. It is amazing that people have gained knowledge of these various plants and flowers that grow so easily all around us. Rosemary is one plant which is associated with a number of legends as well as cures. As usual, Culpepper gives the appropriate celestial influence which is, in this case, none other than the sun. It has a fragrance and a few sprays laid on the breast of a chicken or a leg of lamb does make a difference. Its oil is one of the essential oils used in aromatherapy and I use it frequently when I mix up my lotions and potions which I have to do in the summer when insects torment my Welsh cobs. Of all the wisdom in Culpepper's book, the one which I shall remember is that Rosemary . . . 'is a remedy for windiness of the stomach, bowels and spleen and it expels it powerfully.' Romans wind it in their wreaths which are worn around their heads on special occasions. It is an attractive plant. When it roots and grows it looks healthy and free from most diseases. It is an unusual shade of green which lasts all the year and its shape is the opposite of some straggly shrubs. Even when it becomes fully grown it maintains a good contour and the little flowers which are tiny and pale blue are most delicate.

I read in Culpepper that Mustard grew only in gardens or in well-manured places and somehow he seemed to understand the importance of Mustard as an additive . . . 'to help the digestion of meat for those with weak stomachs' and also as something which will help to draw out splinters and other foreign bodies. It is strange that he touched upon some of the essential properties of this plant without visualising the importance that Mustard would find in our modern lives. For example, the essential differences between English and French Mustard and the number of times it is recommended for inclusion in a recipe. In homes and hospitals a Mustard bath is almost a luxury when one has a bad cold or when there has been exposure to undue frost or damp. He gives it very many virtues. He emphasise heat and relates it to Mars, although he says Aries has something to do with it. For a sore throat he suggests a poultice wrapped around the throat, similar to other means of applying heat which have been told me, for example, a sock filled with salt which has been heated will relieve a sore throat.

John Lust almost agrees with him. He says that mustard is an appetiser but that it is also an irritant. I seem to remember those plasters used to raise heat to a degree which enabled a patient to forget the pain it is meant to relieve. John Lust suggests that it is good for sciatica, rheumatism and many similar aches and pains. This remedy seems to have been forgotten for most things except for the purpose of enhancing a meal and for those Mustard baths.

Ants are held up to us as an example of activity and labour – 'Go to the ant thou sluggard, consider her ways and be wise.'

The Culinary Herbs in our Kitchens

For a moment I shall list some herbs which are used with regularity in the kitchen. Mostly they are fragrant and certain combinations are always successful. Roast lamb and mint for example; pork with Sage and Thyme; Rosemary on a roasted chicken; Horseradish with roast beef.

Most of these herbs will make a pleasant tea which could have a beneficial effect, although it is well to remember that when taken in this way care must be taken for there are dangers. Mint which is an antispasmodic carminative also for nervousness and insomnia and is recommended as a drink twice daily (2-3 leaves in a cup of water) cannot be treated as a summer quaff, if taken for more than a few days might result in heart problems.

Rosemary is recommended mainly for external use, in hair rinses and shampoos and in aromatherapy and excessive use of Thyme could lead to poisoning. As these herbs are hardly ever used in large amounts we need not worry, in our case we pick the odd sprig to lay on our meat prior to roasting or use a commercially prepared product. It is well to remember that most of the herbalists in the Monasteries and those who studied the subject seriously were wise men and women, the beneficial or harmful properties had been known for many years. Sage is linked with wisdom, the name declares this fact. It is said to relieve a headache, but mainly it is an aid to digestion and perhaps this is why Sage and Onion stuffing is used to take the greasiness away from a pork lunch. A friend of mine was told by an old lady when, after childbirth, it was time for her milk to dry off, a bunch of dried Sage tied under her arms would help in this matter. Dried Sage helps to create heat and is also good to keep away moths. It is a useful shrub to have in the herb garden, the leaves are an unusual shade of green and it is always handy to enliven a meal.

As I wrote this I realised that Thyme was an ingredient used, even now, in the gargle Glycerine and Thymol. Those who enjoy a Herb Garden are usually enthusiastic cooks as well as gardeners. The idea is attractive, interesting and a little romantic and most often there is the bonus of scent. Herbs should always grow close to the kitchen and window-sills are useful for this purpose.

There are always people who have listened to all the tales told by the old gardeners. One lady I knew well, full of knowledge about plants and folklore, told me that one must plant Parsley in the first week in June and allow the seed time to go down to the devil and back. However, other gardeners advise that there should be several sowings of Parsley, in April, in July or early August, the last sowing is for a winter supply. We are fortunate to be able to buy it all the year around in the supermarkets, though personal pride gives us satisfaction when we pick our own. Many mystical factors are connected with Parsley. Mrs. M. Grieve says that there is an old superstition which says that Parsley should never be transplanted. The herb itself is said to be dedicated to Persephone and to funeral rites by the Greeks.

In another legend, it is said to have sprung from the blood of a Greek hero, Archemorus, the forerunner of death, and Homer relates that chariot horses were fed by the warriors on the leaves. Greek gardens were bordered with the herbs, Parsley and Rue. Parsley must have an aura of an ancient conflict with evil. In Susan's Campbell's book of *Garden Lore* she tells us that it is best to plant Parsley on Good Friday as of all plants it is the one most affected by the Devil and as she says . . . 'Everyone knows that Good Friday is the one day on which the Devil is powerless.'

I can add only that I love the taste of Parsley, there is a fresh fragrance about it, especially if it is chopped and placed in the pan with butter and new potatoes. In Cornwall, on Wednesdays, when we had our pasty for lunch, my father had a special pasty with Parsley and an egg broken into it.

Culpepper tells us, 'It is very comfortable to the stomach, good for wind and to remove obstructions both of the liver and spleen' . . . Galen commendeth it for the falling sickness . . . the seed is effectual to break the stone and ease the pains and torments thereof . . . the leaves of Parsley laid to the eyes that are inflamed with heat or swollen, relieves them if it be used with bread or meat . . . The juice dropped into the ears with a little wine easeth the pains.'

Apart from our ancient advisor, it is reported that in the trenches, where our men often got kidney complications or suffered from dysentery, Parsley tea was beneficial. It is said that 'whoever grow the Parsley with success will be the leader in the house'. Women are often the most successful. They are then said 'to wear the pants'.

These herbs are our familiar ingredients. I could mention the Bay Tree which is a large tree with nondescript leaves which do add an individual flavour to fish recipes. When boiling a piece of ham I add some Bay leaves (one or two will make all the difference) and Juniper berries which may be obtained in the health shops. On the shelves in most shops which sell food there are little cylinders of dried herbs, although I have lost faith in these lately, probably because fresh herbs are so available.

With the broadening of our horizons and the increase of cookery programmes on radio and television, some herbs which are mentioned in most herbal books, yet were not as available a few years ago, are now being used with more abandon as we cook. For example, Lemon Balm and Basil. I have a strong Lemon Balm but little pots of Basil are very fragile in spite of tender and passionate care. A herb which I have and hardly ever use, for the simple reason it is a little further away from the kitchen, at the end of my patch of herbs, is Borage. I shall replant it and use it much more often. The leaves may be mixed with lettuce leaves, chives and Dandelion leaves with half a thin-skinned orange, unpeeled and finely sliced, a salad dressing made from the usual mixture of vinegar and oil with a little chopped garlic, salt and pepper. It is said by the authors, John and Rosemary Hemphill, the author of *Herbs and Spices*, that a few of the blue flowers which are also edible may be scattered over the top of the salad. Borage is supposed to have a faint cucumber flavour which makes it sound even more refreshing. I can imagine this salad on a summer's day, eaten outside with a slice of cold lamb and lovely fresh-from-the-oven bread rolls. Today, the sun is shining and although the ground remains damp after the recent rain, writing this has made me determined to go out and plant a healthy offshoot of this plant to be within my reach.

I am interested in Rue . . . There is an ambiance which surrounds the plant which threatens. Shakespeare says (from 'Richard III'):

> 'Here in this place
> I'll set a bank of Rue, sour herb of grace;
> Rue, even for Ruth, shall shortly here be seen,
> In remembrance of a weeping Queen.'

Because of its association with repentance, I suppose the saying 'to rue the day' means one will live to regret something or other. Nothing is attractive about Rue. It is smelly and tastes horrible and even when it grows it is awkward and straggly. Once, I was stupid enough to try it – it is not an asset. It is fitting that the one good thing about it is that it kills fleas.

When the family owned a budgerigar we made certain that it had in its cage a small twig of Millet. It cost about 6d (in the old money). Beauty could not get enough of it and most times the seeds were empty and open. Some other seeds were implanted amongst the Millet which were used for growing an illegal plant which seemed harmless. It was fine for Beauty, but it was withdrawn from the market. Poor Beauty, he used to enjoy that spray of seed.

Hemp has the possibility to benefit the medical world. There has been a discovery that there are cannabis receptors in the brain and the research could lead to the discovery of a natural brain chemical which might give the same effect the smoking of Cannabis would have. Perhaps some day the anomalies will be ironed out and a true benefit will be found. Until then, we shall have to obey the law.

I heard a story once about women working in a factory where Hemp was made. The man described such a vivid picture which I could see in my mind that I have never forgotten. I saw a factory which was dingy and dusty and littered with old rope and plants which looked like rope. The colour was tobacco brown and the women who worked on this factory floor merged into the whole scene. Their faces were stained and their clothes were the same colour as the ropes and sacks. They might have been insects camouflaged against a beach or a piece of land . . . We have seen on television those wonderful rope slings which cross deep river beds. Old ropes on ships or ropes used as supports like banisters for stairs. Indian Hemp was originally from Asia, it is cultivated in most temperate countries for its fibres which are found in the outer layer of the stem. Apart from those sturdy ropes, twines, hessian and even linen and lace might be produced. It is only lately that the factory in Dundee where all these things were produced has closed.

In Cannabis the dried leaves and female flowers and resin are used. Cannabis can be smoked or swallowed and has all kinds of effects on the mind which might be pleasant or can even be unpleasant and hallucinatory. It has been very much of our own culture, especially in the Sixties and especially connected with the world of pop music. This is a plant which causes much debate and one day there might be a final verdict regarding its use.

A Wild Corner

'Nettle in, Dock out
Dock rub nettle out.

In reference books it is said that the prolific growth of Nettles around houses and farms is a sign that there has been blood spilt on the land. Nettles grow best where blood has been spilt. Surely around places in farmyards where pigs were killed or carcasses had been buried, etc. this is logical. Stinging Nettles are not to be despised. In *The Modern Herbal* by Mrs. M. Grieves she says, 'the young tops should be gathered when 6-8 inches high. Gloves should be worn to protect hands when being picked. Nettles should be washed in running water with a stick and put into a saucepan whilst still dripping and cooked with the lid on for 20 minutes. Then chopped, rubbed through with a hair-sieve and either served plain or warmed with a little butter, salt and pepper and with or without a poached egg.' The similarity to Spinach is demonstrated here. I feel the recommended 20 minutes cooking time is a little long.

There is a saying, also read in the above book that Campbell wrote, when he complained of how little attention is paid to nettles in England, 'In Scotland I have eaten nettles, I have slept in nettle sheets and I have dined off a nettle tablecloth. The young and tender nettle is an excellent pot herb. The stalks of the old nettle are as good as flax for making cloth. I have heard my old mother say that she thought nettle cloth more durable than any other species of linen.'

In the wild patch there are trees. When we kept goats I loved to gather bundles of their favourite branches to put in racks for their nightly treats. When there was a choice they would nibble the branches from the Ash tree first.

Ash was their favourite, then they would choose Oak, Hawthorn and Beech and anything else I could find in the hedgerow which I could be certain were not poisonous. I would love to have set the goats free but they had to be tied, they were notorious escapees and made for the garden where there were dangerous shrubs. Goats seemed to have no discernment at all. Most evergreens are dangerous, if not lethal.

Goats are fascinating. At times the idea of using a pet goat as a mower of unwanted plants is irresistible but, apart from eating the treasured plants and spoiling the herbaceous border, their waywardness is too powerful. Goats are the poor man's Jersey cow. This is seen on our television screens when there are pictures of less developed countries when a herd of goats is obviously a part of the nation's economy. One more fact on their benefit to man, it is said, I have not tried it yet, though it makes sense, that to hollow out a pellet of goat's dung, insert a seed of whatever, Eocket, Endive, Cress or Lettuce the seed will thrive exceedingly. This information came from Pliny who died in A.D.79.

Sometimes animals seek and will find their remedy. We rub nettle stings with Dock leaves instinctively; an older horse or one who suffers from a little heart failure will nibble at Ivy leaves. The literature from most books about Ivy tell us that Ground Ivy is a diuretic, astringent and gently stimulant, but has little to say about the well-known climbing Ivy except that it is decorative on the walls of old houses. The Old Queen Mary was famous for her condemnation of the plant for the opposite reason. Personally, I like it, for me it has held together some of my own old walls.

In the wild corner there is a profusion of plants which must have been used in the past and which we have ignored. Such knowledge will have to be rediscovered.

Dandelions, first one or two and later, a spread of gold across the lawn, which would make us exclaim with wonder if it was not a weed. Later, I shall expect to see families of goldfinches, dipping and darting across our patch . . . rare birds and appearing just at this time. I wonder is this why they are called Goldfinches, as if there is an infinity, these birds use also the down from Coltsfoot to line their nests. Bullfinches will swing amongst the branches of our Fushia bush later in the year.

We called Dandelions 'Pee the bed' and it answered important questions as we blew the light as Thistledown seeds from a rounded head of fluff, an occasion when our own folklore was not far off the mark for it is recorded in many herbal books that the Dandelion is a diuretic. Even Culpepper wrote, 'It openeth the passages of urine in both young and old; powerfully cleanseth impostumes and inward ulcers in the urinary passages, and by its drying and temperate quality doth afterwards heal them; for which purpose the decoction of the roots or leaves in white wine, or the leaves chopped as pot-herbs, with a few Lisanders, and boiled in their broth, are very effectual.'

Mrs. M. Grieve – *A Modern Herbal* – gives the following information.

In this book there are almost twelve columns of closely written text regarding the Dandelion or its French 'Dent de Lion' from which the name has been corrupted. This gives too much detail for my report, but 'Its medicinal action and uses . . . Diuretic, tonic and slightly aperient. It is a general stimulant to the system, but especially to the urinary organs and is chiefly used in liver and kidney disorders.' Kidney taken as proved, but 'for liver? Is there a hint of associated mirror magic? The yellow plant and a state of biliousness?'

I know Dandelion and Burdock were the favourite drinks from the weekly Corona delivery when I was young. Dandelions have been well documented and Burdock an ingredient in many recipes. I do not find a lot to say about Burdock, I suppose it is famous for those little burrs we hated so much in our courting days.

Around the abandoned logs where there are crannies which sprout baby ferns; rough patches of bark where insects shelter, small holes for all kinds of creatures to escape the all-seeing yellow eyes of the night owls, lichen and once I discovered a strange, pale green plant which I had seen somewhere previously. I guessed it was Sphagnum Moss and later this was verified. I would not disclose this area to anyone . . . even my friends, many of them are botanists and they are least likely to trust. They are collectors, the ones who think, 'One little snippet of this plant would not hurt.' They take it from its environment where it has thrived for years and it disappears. Perhaps a lille personal advantage might result from this interest. Penicillin which changed for ever our treatment of illness and injury was discovered by Alexander Fleming in 1941 when he noticed the area around the green mould on a piece of cheese was not decomposing as was the rest of the portion. This was an agent which killed bacteria. Later the whole concept was developed so that micro-organisms could be attacked in a specific manner.

My first introduction to Sphagnum Moss was in 1940 when I was doing my nursing training. It was during the war but much of the nursing practices belonged to the twenties and thirties. There were even leeches kept for observation in the laboratory as proof that they had been used. Actually, modern medicine has found a use for them since. The slabs of Sphagnum Moss were used to pack around the plastic containers used for the after treatment in prostetectomies. The containers were not flexible enough to fit adequately. The dressing seeped through to the sheets and the rest of the bed. We tried to get these patients seen to as soon as it was daylight. A necessity to wash and powder and change all the bedding took so much time, at that time Sphagnum Moss was a boon. Its ability to absorb moisture saved such a lot. It could have been a sponge, an application from nature itself. Now I have learnt a little of the history of Sphagnum I know from recorded history that it has been used since 1014. It was a global remedy, cases from Kashmiri and Laplanders, Highlanders and Eskimos were to benefit from its sponge-like absorption of fluid from wounds. Animals also learnt that if they were wounded and lay in a bed of this cushion-like plant their blood would be stanched and possibly they might survive.

It was collected from the bogs in large slabs which were left to dry in the sun and the wind. They were turned on each successive day until completely dry. They were then cut into squares which were covered in muslin to be used as dressings. It was useful that they could be reused many times. At a later stage it was used in conjunction with the juice expressed from a clove of garlic which meant an antiseptic dressing was available. Because it is renewable it is now grown commercially. To reassure patients please note that modern operations are much less complicated by this prolonged after-care and much less time has to be spent in hospitals. During ancient battles it is possible to imagine how they could be used to good effect. Other plants came into their own at these times, Plantain could be used to stop bleeding when someone has a cut. If a wound is deeper, a handful of cobwebs could be crushed into the wound. The Physicians of Myddfai discovered the value of cobwebs and there was always Comfrey.

So many remedies around us yet Penicillin was the missing element. It made such a difference to all routines in a hospital. Perhaps there was a tendency to depend on it too much. We knew that cross-infection was less of a danger when this powerful antibiotic was present and the constant boiling of steel kidney dishes and syringes (which were not disposable); the pressure steam methods of sterilizing drums of varied dressings ceased. All that was necessary was to change the pack for whichever treatment on the trolley.

When so many plants grow in a patch of earth which has not been organised only those who are really knowledgeable are able to appreciate their values. I think of a text book I had once which has been lost. It was a thin black book which contained a wealth of knowledge about the varied flora in the tropical forests of Central America. At the time I was surprised to learn of how many of these plants were used in modern medicine, for example there was the plant from which we obtained Cocaine and many others. Even then we were exploiting the people and the forests of Brazil and recently there was a programme about this subject which said how much more we are discovering about the seeds and the barks of trees and different plants. The medicinal value is fully realised by the firms which manufacture our own medicines and their superior knowledge gives them such an advantage. Their aim is to patent for themselves the discovery and knowledge gained by the native population. We must mention the number of patches of Snowdrops and of Bluebells found in our wild corners.

The missing factor of course is the availability of antibiotics. Most remedies are around us but for serious infection there had to be discovery of the century . . . antibiotics. In hospitals we began to depend on the new wonderful drugs which resisted infection, yet soon the bacteria began to put up their own resistance.

There is a plant which I have heard about for many years but it was a recent programme on television that I heard something which I found interesting. I took great interest in the remedy one gardener was passing on to another regarding a positive cure for ants (or for their extermination). He said if some Penny Royal was planted close to the area for protection, ants would never invade. There was something in the plant which they hated. As I am plagued each year when the weather is extra hot with a raid from an outside source right into the house, I was interested. I was sure I had some Penny Royal growing quite near and I began investing its properties in my books. I discovered in a book by Roy Genders, *The Scented Wild Flowers of Britain*, that Penny Royal, found on moist heathlands and pastures and on the banks of brooks was named by Pliny, for it was in great demand because of ridding a house of fleas. The Royal addition given to the name was because it was also used in their residences for this purpose. Not only houses but it was sold in the streets of London, mostly to sailors to sweeten their drinking water whilst at sea and also to rid their quarters of fleas. Well . . . if it is good enough for fleas, what will it do for ants?

The Green Land

I could not hear them as they worked
in the last field at Tŷ'n y Cwm
when the sun was a flaring ball
resting on the edge of a hay-scented world.
So many times I crossed the top lane
then back to the kitchen and
the throaty tick of the old clock
and Mamgu's stories.

Then, nearing midnight I crossed
the top lane, the air was moist
and the glare of the sun was remembered
by gold streaks in the sky. I heard
a whir of a slow engine and shouts
of the late hay makers. I returned
to the kitchen. The tick of the clock quickened
and the tales of the old lady
became new commands

Memory brings this scene to life. It was a summer's evening and the farmer at Disgwylfa was turning the cut grass in the large field which lay beneath the woodland on his farm. I was riding my mare Honey around the headings. The cut grass lay in green swathes and shone in the last of the sunlight. It was slippery I recall and I was careful when my mare drew too close to the 'killed' grass. Light, scent, sound and sight combined in that moment.

I noticed how the light tractor, with the whirling machine behind, sent grass flying and the ancient straw hat which had been taken from its hook on the timbers of the kitchen ceiling was worn by David Jones, farmer. Underneath was a large cabbage leaf which stopped him having a headache. At the time, for me, this was a new idea. It made sense. Later, I realised it could be used with as much effect as a poultice to draw out a strain or pain in a knee. Someone said it made a very soothing poultice for mastitis. It is the heat which soothes but some substance such as cabbage or bran or bread or linen with camomile holds the heat for longer.

There is a good recipe for an ointment made from Mallow in the old W.I. book I mentioned which is good for bruises, also the following from the *Herbal* by Mrs. M. Grieves:

> An ointment made from Marsh Mallow has also a popular reputation but it is stated that a poultice made of the fresh root, with the addition of a little white bread proves more serviceable when applied externally than the ointment. The fresh leaves steeped in hot water and applied to the affected parts as a poultice, also reduced inflammation and bruised and rubbed upon any place stung by wasps or bees take away the pain, inflammation and swelling. Pliny stated that the green leaves, beaten with nitre and applied drew out thorns and prickles in the flesh.

At this stage I will say that an ointment which is effective and I would use happily on any cut or sore which does not need an antibiotic, Calendula ointment or Marigold ointment is one which I would choose.

Wintergreen, with the strong smell of all liniments, is used for strains. I have seen the bruise appear almost at the same time as the ointment is applied. This is the smell present in sporting dressing-rooms. A smell which gives confidence.

I have been told that this smell is associated with dressing-rooms associated with most sporting activities. A hot bath soaks away pain and the smell of liniment, Methyl Salicylate or Wintergreen, will forever remind them of triumph or disaster.

In our house there was always a bottle of Camphorated Oil. I have written already about the smell and the glowing comfort after an application. It is interesting to note the common ingredients of the above examples taken from the Cornish book of recipes, vinegar, turpentine, eggs, ducks or hens as long as they were fresh. The one exotic addition was 1 pennyworth tincture of Myrrh. A description of Myrrh taken from the *Herb Book* by John Lust, which is a mine of information, says that Myrrh is the aromatic, gummy substance exuded by certain trees and shrubs growing in eastern Africa and Arabia. The three wise men who travelled afar to give their gifts in the stable at Bethlehem have made us all aware of this fact. It is said to be an antiseptic, astringent, carminative, stomachic. It makes a good gargle and mouthwash for sore and throat, sore teeth and gums, coughs, asthma and other chest problems. It is one of those all powerful gifts to mankind.

Turpentine is an ingredient used often in animal liniments. This is a harsh addition – often used in home-made remedies sold in horse sales or markets. They do work, some people use them rather than milder versions.

There is always Vick in its blue bottle jar.

I have rubbed Vick on my Mother's chest during her last years whenever she was 'chesty'. I have put some in boiling water and inhaled whenever I have felt my own breathing a bit blocked. I always have it in my own cupboard. So much green and we realise that not only emeralds are precious.

A trestle table outside with chairs for the family and the habit of eating in the fresh air is a dream which dissipates when clouds form on summer days. We can envy those Mediterranean scents and joyful meals when everyone seems about to burst into song, yet our green world supplies food and medicine and feeds thousands of our animals through the year.

Think of the scent of dried grass when hay is gathered in for winter fodder and consider our lovely vegetables, the Cornish Broccoli, Pembrokeshire potatoes, Jersey potatoes; Watercress and, above all, our Savoy Cabbages. We may not have eternal sunshine but we do have changing seasons There are the Hazel Nuts and Blackberries; Whinberries and Mushrooms and in our hedgerows many of the plants I have mentioned. We have relied for many years on the Cabbage, it seemed always to be on the edge of our plates since we were children, often left there. I think of the Savoy because of its large and succulent leaves.

I think of David Jones when he placed a cabbage leaf under his hat to cure a headache or to cool his head when he worked in the hot sun and of others who use it as a poultice to ease mastitis or to draw out inflammation from a painful joint. I like to drink the water in which a cabbage was boiled, there is no accounting for tastes but I consider it delicious. Just now in this context I will give a recipe discovered in research, which I have not tried but which I feel in my bones would give real relief. These are the details taken from *Grandmother's Secrets* by Jean Palaiseul. It was advocated in the eighteenth century, probably one of those cures handed from family to family. It goes under the name of 'Boerhaave Syrup' and is reckoned to be a secret remedy for consumption. Take a tablespoonful of red cabbage syrup . . . this is made from about five or six red cabbage leaves which have been pounded in a mortar to extract the juice, the mixture squeezed hard through a muslin cloth will ensure that as much as possible of the main ingredient is extracted, weigh the juice and add half its weight in honey and cook in a gentle heat, skimming as necessary until it acquires the consistency of syrup. For persons with a weak chest, one tablespoonful taken first thing every morning it will also be a preventative medicine. As I write this I would think the quantities should be increased to ensure at least one full bottle will be prepared so that it could often be repeated.

Cabbage is associated with many minerals. We were told to eat up your cabbage as children. By making it compulsory, our parents made us resent this dark green vegetable, which threatened us by the all pervading smell which heralded its appearance. I take care these days as I cook Cabbage, yet it is difficult. Recently, I saw on television an expert on the benefits of herbs and healthy eating pronounce the Cabbage as his most important plant. There must be something unusual in the constituents of this plant for my mares, who eat most vegetables and green plants, do not like Brassica Oleracea and if it is included in their pan of food it is left while the last of apple shreds or carrots are licked clean. This proves the delicate balance of nature and the difference in the needs of all living creatures.

Comfrey is well-known for its medicinal properties. In the old days a supply of branches and leaves were given room on a ship as a remedy for many different afflictions. It is such an unprepossessing little plant, strong and healthy and able to hold its own in a garden but . . . nothing much to look at. The name given it 'Knitbone' is significant. I swear by it and always have a jar of this black ointment near by. It feels so safe and one is able to smear it over a cut liberally and I have used it often.

Other greens, Watercress and Spinach, are rich in calcium, copper and potassium as well as iodine. A Watercress sandwich with salt and pepper with fresh bread is always acceptable. Carrots produce lovely feathery leaves which are attractive and on a market stall they add to the appearance of the vegetable. Some people prefer their carrots without these leaves, maybe for economical reasons and perhaps they are not good for us. I always choose them if they are available as they are a treat for the mares. It is true that a carrot in the horse world is as effective as a banana seems to be in the world of the monkeys and, currently, in the word of the athletes. The juice and the vegetable are seriously valuable. When I worked in a Medical Centre in the Gwendraeth Valley the man who sold vegetables at the gate on pay days always gave me bags of carrots which were past their first freshness. They have been grown as fodder for animals for many years and at the present time there are few people who do not appreciate and enjoy a carrot.

All this against a background of woodlands and fields and our marshlands must make our country one of the richest in the world. Yes, we know about the rain and the wind.

We have seen a fern growing. Some have been lucky enough to see its imprint on a shining piece of anthracite found underneath the ground when they have been working as miners. This makes one realise how enduring the frail plant is and how nothing is ever really lost. It is wise to think of the fossils when we think of our plants. I have collected one or two examples and have seen some perfect things. The sides of a tree with all its vertical ridges (which could be lethal if it fell underground when disturbed), a shell and I remember one description given to me by a miner when he said that the sides of the coal-face underground at a particular spot looked as if it had been papered with a picture of a green valley. Ferns must be the most ancient of our heritage. Its pattern is definite. I have been shown it so often and seen its imprint on anthracite which have been collected for me by the miners. Such a variety of ferns and bracken once covered the valleys and hillsides. There is the Royal Fern, once indicated to me with so much pride by a friend who was a distinguished botanist in the area. The correct name of this species is Osmunda Regalis. I knew exactly where this fern grew and it answers the kind of soil which suits it most, a soil composed of ancient bog land and earth. The name is derived from Osmund, and the white centres of its roots have been called the heart of Osmund. A legend which is connected with the fern is that the wife and daughter of Osmund, a waterman of Lock Tyne, took refuge among Osmundes during an invasion of the Danes. Osmund is a Saxon word for domestic peace, another theory is that the name Osmunda comes from the god Thor and some have connected it to an ability to cleanse. This might relate to some of the medicinal qualities of the fern or perhaps to the action of water passing through its leaves as that water is sieved. Whatever . . . it is the tallest and obviously the most regal of our ferns and it is only right that all these stories have grown around it. Many of its medicinal qualities are similar to other ferns and perhaps it is well to leave Osmunda Regalia in her own romantic setting. Other ferns will do for their more practical qualities.

There is the Male Fern. Gerard wrote, 'The roots of the Male Fern, being taken in the weight of ½ driveth forth long flat worms.' This has been mentioned earlier in the book and many of the ferns are described as anthelmintics. Another use for this fern and probably the female fern and many others in common with Bracken is that, having been burnt the ashes are used in the manufacture of making glass or soap.

Most farmers hate Bracken, it takes over acres of land and is said, with authority, to contain a carcoginious substance which is fatal to sheep. I have been riding my mare along a path where Bracken grows and she loved to snatch at a long piece of Bracken which was impossible for her to swallow at once. She used to enjoy tossing it around in the same way as a child waves a rattle or a stick. Bracken has one use which I think would make it worth while and that when it is burnt the smoke drives away all those irritating gnats, other insects and, even snakes . . . 'and other noisome creatures,' says Culpepper. There is the long-tongued Hart's Fern. This is seen frequently in the lanes around our house. The name echoes the shape of the fern which is fairly long and the frond is not divided. One use is made of this plant apart from an old remedy mentioned by Galen is that it makes an infusion which is effective against diarrhoea and, dysentery is that an ointment which may be used for burns, scalds and piles . . . anything which is sore and painful. Because of a long association with all kinds of fern, people must have learnt to become dependent on its virtues as a result of studying the plant. It has many uses, at times bracken is cut in the autumn with the *Brwyn* and it is useful for bedding for the animals.

There is one park which I loved. It was on the sea-front at Falmouth. There was a grassy mound with a small granite post and if I stood in this spot I had a spiritual sensation. Just inside the lower entrance there was an excavation which might have once been a quarry yet it was created for the large Australian Fern which, from its origin in the centre had taken over the whole area. Probably it is still there, maybe one day I shall return to see. I mention it to explain just how old and powerful this group of plants is and how the varieties are bound to make a difference to our lives. Even Mare's Tail, or Fox's Tail which is the bane of gardeners' lives has a use. At one time before shopping at the supermarkets made life easier, a handful of this plant would be used to scour the inside of saucepans after a meal.

A permanent inhabitant of the green world is the Ivy. It grows on an old tree which I see every day. I do not now whether the tree supports the Ivy or the Ivy holds the tree together. I only know that amongst all those leaves there are hundreds of birds, some of which I never see. Of course, there are the old favourites, they fly near whenever I open the back door. I see an old crow who uses one of the top branches for a perch. A crow is not everyone's companion I know, but I feel sorry for it, standing on its branch, bare in winter, with its feathers, as they are blown back by the wind showing how white it is becoming. In summer near the top there is a robin which sings its heart out. Late autumn and we notice Ivy is the last plant to yield some honey for bees and the wildlife around must be grateful. One thing I have to report about the Ivy that I have not seen in any of the reference books: I have heard it mentioned at times and I have noted it in a previous chapter that when a horse is old, maybe just tired or maybe suffering from an incipient heart trouble, it will go out of its way to nibble at an ivy leaf. This, which might be dismissed as ground cover, is not just that. The factor which makes me think it will work was a paragraph in Jean Palaiseul's book, *Grandmother's Secrets*. In this section Ivy is invaluable when there are inflammatory conditions . . . cellulitis and rheumatic swellings, sciatica and similar external ailments. When there is undue heat in the tissues which has to be drawn out from the body ivy leaves will make a hot poultice. An advantage is the abundance of growth and its presence in each season. An extra advantage is that its application does not involve any 'Mumbo Jumbo' as my friend, the pharmacist, would say. What it entails is the gathering of fresh leaves, either chopped, which would release more juices, or crushed, heated and applied to the skin, naturally on a piece of linen which would be bandaged in place. A second method is to take two handfuls of such leaves and mix them with 4 oz Bran with hot water, thereby making a simple poultice which would have an extra long period of heat.

There is a primitive form of first-aid when the juice of an Ivy leaf (Ground Ivy in this case) is chewed by the owner of a wounded Cock in a Cock fight and spat into that wounded eye. It should heal. All this indicates there are properties which may be beneficial other than a means to apply heat. I have a leg which does swell and become inflamed at periods, it would not do any harm to give the above treatment a try.

In my mind there has always been conflict between the drawing out of inflammation by means of heat and the subduing of it by means of an injection of an antibiotic . . . which means no poultices at all. Whilst working in the Medical Centre this meant that even the treating of a septic finger was a matter for some thought. Penicillin was the magic cure. Now time has proved that super bugs will appear to overcome a new enemy. Doctors are reluctant to prescribe antibiotics for this reason and of course there is the over-stretching of the health service.

Some plants are framed in their individual mystique. Lime, dedicated to Venus. Saint Hildegard warded off plagues with a ring with a green stone, beneath which was a fragment of Lime wrapped in a spider's web.

Lime evokes a cool atmosphere . . . equals a remedial effect on epilepsy and I associate it with that background of shining leaves which counteracts heat on a summer's day at Wimbledon.

Flag Iris (Iris Pseudacorus).

Primrose (Primula Vulgaris).

Clover (Pink & White). Trifolium Repens/Trifolium Pratense (Pink).

Poppy and Foxgloves.

Gorse.

Rose Hips (Rosa Canina).

Crack Willow.

Wild Arum (Arum Maculatum).

Water Cress, Flag Iris and Willow Herb.

Hawthorn.

Honeysuckle (Lonicera Perickymenum).

Convolvulus (Calystegia Sepium).

Kingcups (Caltha Palustris).

Spindle Berries (Evonymus Europaeus).

Bluebell Wood, Wranaton.

Meadowsweet.

Gwaunydd Cochion/Tumble Mire

Referring to the list of the plants found in this area, many were classified. Now I realise how secret were their habitats. I had walked so many times around this peatland area, which we call the mountain walk, with Mr. Chips, my Golden Labrador and had no idea of the scientific importance of this site . . . nor of its secrets. For me, it was a lovely area of red and mauve. Each path seemed to have its significance and I remember how Mr. Chips used to bound ahead of me to splash through the ditches and streams which criss-crossed the walk.

So many of the plants had a medicinal value that I wonder if its vicinity to the hospital had influenced the building of it on that particular site. I also remember in those first years an abundance of the giant Buttercup which grew around an attractive ditch, almost a pool.

In late summer, this spot was God's own rockery . . . Heather and the Rosebay Willow seeming to be planted by an artist. A walk which had to be shared. On one occasion I had to go back and bring an elderly neighbour close to the scene so that she could see for herself what I had described so often.

On another occasion, as I stood at the gate of the hospital which was opposite the entrance of the path which led across the mountain, I heard the following words in my mind, the hospital at the time was a hospital reserved for the care of the elderly and was a sanctuary for those who needed long term care in the adjoining mining village:

ON SUCH A NIGHT

It had spread before so many eyes,
this fecund peatland. God's Rockery,
in sunlight when the hidden fern or heather
reflects the carmine glow which named it
Gwaunydd Cochion.

So many times I listened to its music,
the incessant skylark's song in summer,
in winter, the stormy sound of wind,
nothing stops the elemental spirit of the moor,

not when the Rosebay willow herb fills
all hollows with its foliage

or crackling fires in spring which sear
the mind . . . the black to make the green.

I had watched often but never
seen it as on this night . . . balmy
with the first scents of summer,
all colours and shadows . . . flickering
in a sinking sun.
I saw it with such yearning.

As those who watched from gentle windows
the moor, which comforted the fading lives of those
who boned the fabric of the Gwendraeth
fleshed the streets with hope and laughter,
who burrowed deep in those rich veins
which still remain a part, as the wiry Mare's Tail.

I saw it on that evening . . . and stood in silence.

I began with that memory . . . This was world of purple Moorgrass, Bullrushes and the Rosebay Willow . . . Gwaunydd Cochion, so rightly named.

There is a history of favourite remedies and applications in all parts of the British Isles. I know this from family stories, sometimes they related anecdotes of encounters with, for example and without intention to make them seem outside the human race, odd characters brought up by the sea or on farms, gypsies, blacksmiths, even the odd artist, but personalities who owed to their roving existence or the exact opposite, genuine knowledge, tried and tested. Knowledge which a chance of a conversation might give an opportunity for that knowledge to be perpetuated.

Credit must be given to the environment and in the fertile lands of Carmarthenshire there has been an abundance and variety of plants which has enhanced the knowledge of local people. Some of whom, as we will realise in the following chapters, have expressed an interest in the medicinal properties of plants.

In about 1220 there was a wise and far-seeing Prince of South Wales who realised the combination of knowledge, energy, motivation and environmental advantages of a certain family who became known and famous through the centuries as 'The Physicians of Myddfai'. The father Rhiwallon and his three sons, Cadwgan, Gruffudd and Einion, were patronised by this Prince so that they could 'without molestation or interruption attend to the study of their profession and administer relief to such as applied to them.' (*Welsh Botanology*, 1813) The study of Botanology became one of the three sciences, the others Theology and Astronomy.

From here onwards the collecting and use of plants were bound up with medicine and probably Monks and other learned people helped to promote the healing by means of their own hands-on methods.

The author of *The Magic of Herbs*, David Conway, spoke of rather an unattractive male whose appearance and matching vile language must have made him someone to fear. This factor, most often, is used against a female healer, a white witch kind of herbalist. It has nothing to do with 'presence'.

I mention this fact because I do not think I am the only person who has discovered an interest in the practical or magical use of plants as a result of the power in a personality. At times this person might be a frail, poor and often ugly, old lady, the kind that so often has been dismissed as mentioned above a witch. It is a kind of wisdom that exudes from these people which commands respect. Something authority in the voice or in the fixing of a gaze.

So often, especially in rural areas, such a wise person claims to be a descendant of 'The Physicians of Myddfai'.

I first heard the story of these physicians years ago when I first came to Wales. I was working in Adelina Patti's home in Breconshire, Craig-y-nos. It was then a sanitarium. It has since become, more in keeping, an musical centre. It was a fleeting reference yet sufficient for me to recognise the story whenever I heard it. Just now as I search through so many books to see which facts link together in the story of the plants and herbs in Wales, I recognise the importance of their influence and am able to understand why legend has overtaken the truth.

In every community there is the Wise One. In Wales the story of the Myddfai physicians retains a powerful hold on the imagination. Maybe the authentic version is the one quoted above from the *Carmarthenshire Antiquarian Magazine*, 1959. It sounds right, a Prince bestowing his patronage, the ancient version of obtaining a franchise on a commodity. Maybe even this has an aura of a legend yet is not a fairy-tale. This

Prince entrusted the father and three sons with a responsibility for the health and care of his subjects. Perhaps the beneficiaries might have been the elite. Whatever that truth, it is the passing down of their knowledge, from father to son through the generations that the essential factor that there would always be someone a Physician, perhaps a doctor, perhaps one of the really 'wise men' on active service in the contemporary community. The example described by David Conway of an uncouth person in appearance and language, a widower, always referred to as Mr. James Tan y' rallt, kept a farm on Plynlimon, a rim of desolate hills. He was tall, enormously stout and clad always in brown tweed. This is a different image from the female version of a wise woman. She has not often the luxury of owning a farm. Most probably she lives in one of those typical rural, cone-shaped hovels. The roof thatched, walls covered in twining foliage, ivy or honeysuckle (typical of a Celtic pattern) or maybe wild roses. Probably there is a small garden for her Parsley, Rosemary, Penny-wort and Fennel. Her knowledge is also handed down. Perhaps she is the seventh daughter of a seventh daughter. She makes sorties into the woods, always a treasure-trove of plants and for the knowledgeable, with medicinal virtues. Once more I think of the terrible destruction of the forests and how, in contrast, this gentle use of plants around the domestic area is natural and essential. There is still so much to discover even in our small world.

The Physicians of Myddfai had their treasures in the fertile soils of South Wales, Breconshire was the scene of the legend, but in the more factual *Carmarthenshire Antiquarian*, it is the rich land around Llandovery, The Tawe, Carmarthen and Llandeilo where their plants were analysed. It is fascinating to note that Middleton Hall which is being changed from a derelict Mansion with neglected grounds into one of the marvels of our own life times. For the record, note, this was opened to the public on June 28th, 2000. It will be as rich in variety and exotic as Kew Gardens. For in this ambitious scheme, greenhouses plants are being transported from all over the world. In spite of this grand source, the creators aim to represent only naturalistic blocks of woodland and moorland from areas of the world with climates similar to that of West Wales. In the Victorian years when large landowners competed with each other for the rare and exotic the tender tropical plants, anything which might prove difficult was collected in world travels. The project at Middleton is created to counteract the havoc which has been done for all the wrong motives. The Director of Horticulture in the National Botanic Garden of Wales worked with those who had environmental awareness much in mind. After the Rio Earth Summit in Brazil the decision was to work to conserve the dwindling natural resources of Planet Earth to leave the world in a fit state for our children to inherit. The competitive urge was suppressed. The threatened ecosystems on the planet which provide habitats are having a second chance. I wonder what the botanists who researched the area around Carmarthenshire earlier in the century would think . . . how much they themselves would be able to contribute with their hard-earned knowledge and how they would be rewarded. And surely the spirit of the Physicians of Myddfai must approve.

The story we read in most books is set in the parish of Myddfai, Llanddeusant, Carmarthenshire. I take the details from a little book, *The Herbal Remedies of the Physicians of Myddfai.* The legend was collected in the year 1841 from oral tradition which still survives amongst some of the older inhabitants of the parishes of Myddfai and Llanddeusant. It was through this same oral tradition that I first heard the story. I can see a face, fervent as if daring me to disbelieve, as she told me . . . more or less the following.

She told that as the struggle to preserve independence of the country was drawing to a close in the 12th century, there lived in Blaensawddle, near Llanddeusant, a widowed woman, she is described, rather poignantly, in this book as a widow of a farmer who had been reduced to harship and poverty through a seris of disastrous circumstances. Providence smiled upon her, and despite her forlorn condition, her livestock had so increased in the course of time that there was insufficient pasture on her own farm. She had to send some of her cattle to graze on the adjoining Black Mountain. As cattle are prone to do, they choose their favourite places and one of these was near a small lake called Llyn y Fan Fach on the north-western side of the Carmarthenshire farm.

Her son grew up to manhood and most of his time was spent in the care of his mother's cattle. One day, as he walked along the edge of the lake, he saw a Lady, sitting on the unruffled surface of the water. Her beauty, in the traditional manner of all fairy-stories, was more than mortal eyes had ever seen. Her hair flowed in ringlets over her shoulders and she combed it, using the glassy surface of the lake as a mirror. She saw the young man who could not take his eyes from her and as she looked, he offered her the one gift he had, his lunch, a humble meal of cheese and barley bread. She had glided towards him and showed interest, but refused his offering as she said, 'Hard baked is thy bread, 'tis not easy to catch me.'

She then dived under the water and disappeared. The love-stricken youth was bewildered. Such a beautiful maiden could never compare with any he was ever likely to meet. He told his mother who saw the effect of the incident on her son. 'It must be the bread. Next time, off her some unbaked bread.' Subsequently this was refused.

This story proceeded as expected. When the fairest of maidens took the bread which was neither too hard baked nor too raw, she agreed to marry him. Her father appeared from the Lake. Instead of a normal father giving away his daughter as a bride, he said, the boy could marry with as many cattle as she could count with one breath as her dowry but . . . to remember that if he were to strike her for no reason three times, she would return to the lake with all her stock.

Magical traditions were woven into this story; the use of the number three; the fact that one black calf which was slaughtered returned to life in order to follow the unreal herd back into the lake after, so inadvertently the omen of striking her three times was fulfilled. There was the presence of three sons.

The importance of this legend lay in the occasional visit of the Lady of the Lake, the fairy-tale mother by this time, who spoke to her sons and gave her gift to them. This was the knowledge of and here I will use the Physicians' own term, the virtue of the herbs and their appearance and properties.

Thus the original physicians, the father and the three sons, their learning of the herbal qualities in the chosen plants and the promise that their name and the name of their descendants would be famous down through the ages and they would be able, through their knowledge, to take away misery and ease the pain of those in their communities.

So the practical and the mythical versions of the responsibility for future medicinal knowledge of the famous physicians have been mentioned. In most books their advice is accompanied by warnings that some cures contain plants which might even be poisonous.

I do not mean the names of their original eleven names are wrong, but some of the mixtures advocated must not be tried. As I have done with the choice from the Druids and shall do with my own favourites, I will try to work out how their plants share praise from many authorities who have written on this subject. In some cases modern scientific knowledge has given authenticity to theories and myths.

This story grew from a myth, yet in the eleventh century one particular family was associated and subsequently connected with the birth of medicine. The non-imaginative consider the truth to be that Rhiwallon and his sons were the first to commit to writing what had been the oral tradition of handing down medicinal secrets from one generation to the next . . . as do all Celts.

One plant which has priority in the Myddfai category is Vervain. It is low in the alphabetical list and does not seem to have any real virtue. Yet as readers will see later this particular plant was credited with strange and mystical qualities, although not considered with as much reverence, now made almost sacred. Vervain, for a long while was the foremost of magical herbs. It was said that those who are rubbed with this will obtain all that they ask. It will cure fevers and cause one person to love another besides curing all kinds of illnesses. Various sources are presented as to the naming of this plant. Romans dedicated it to Venus, Veneris herbal, Veneris Vena . . . luck of Venus. I prefer the Celtic origin, it seems to make more sense and links it more definitely to Druidism . . . *fer faen*, to drive away a stone. Romans offered nosegays of the plant, it was steeped in water at banqueting halls and Druids, before offering sacrifices would wash their altars with Vervain. This would be composed of an infusion of Vervain flowers. It was an ingredient in most love philters and held to be no less effectual in other extremes, for example against the venom of dangerous beasts and serpents and as an antidote against drinks which were bewitched. The Druid priests wore a crown Vervain and in other cases it was worn as a necklace. As in many cases the wild version is richer. This, however, is not all. there was a time when there was a surplus of snakes. Thomas Hardy gives a horrible account of the rural people ridding the area of snakes in his *Return Of The Native* and in Robert Hunt's *Popular Romances of The West* which delves very deeply into this kind of story, there is a piece which describes how these creatures which were in great abundance were dispatched in a similar manner. Somehow Vervain comes into this process. The Druids used to make a circle of Vervain around two snakes which would make them kill each other. There was an accent on circles, a circle around one snake would cause it to die and a simple method of encircling an adder with an image of a circle links this to the story of a circle of Vervain placed around the two snakes. But it is the twining of a pattern around or inside a circle which makes Celtic art distinctive. It is a dominant theme in the style of their jewellry and ironwork. As I write virtue, I wonder about the way it is described in the *Herbal Remedies of the Physicians of Myddfai*, which was translated by

Dr. Derek Bryce and published by Llanerch Enterprises, Felinfach, Lampeter. There is some prominence given to the interpretation of the word 'Virtue.' The herbs described must have included their non-material attributes. He explains that ancient medicines included treatment at a spiritual level and, psychic levels as well as bodily. This is where trust and faith is important, some people say mind over matter and others a 'will to overcome'; modern physicians talk of psychosomatic symptoms.

I have taken a list from David Conway's book, *The Magic Herbs*, of the plants with their special 'virtues' described by the physicians. It will be interesting to compare these with lists in later pages.

There is much written on the latter. It is highly regarded by many nationalities, cultivated in monasteries. Drives away devils and despair. Vettonica . . . Celtic word 'bew'. Romans sprinkled it on the altars of Jupiter and it was employed in rites of love and as mentioned, a sacred plant of the Druids. Latter-day magicians wear a crown of Vervain as protection during the evocation of demons. For centuries Vervain has led the botanical field in the treatment of nervous disorders, epilepsy and asthma. It also fortifies the liver, heart and spleen, relieves mental strain and helps cure infectious diseases (a wine-glassful of a standard infusion, made from the flowers, leaves and diced stalk should be taken on rising). The infusion may be used as a gargle or mouth-wash for sore throats and gums or as an eye lotion of considerable merit. Albertus Magnus calls this her 'pisterion' and recommends it for curing inflammation and diseases of the skin. It is an efficient vermifuge.

Llannon and the Druid Connection

If I had to choose a part of the world where I would have the least of expectation of beauty and excitement I might have considered the parish of Llannon.

Because this book is about discovery and a search for secrets from the land and surrounding environment, it was bound to effect myself when I came to live in the area.

Each place has a history and produces its own evidence. It is not difficult to pin point the highlights in a town. There could be a mediaeval castle, a bridge, names of sites commemorating battles or personalities; such examples are Petticoat Lane, Black Friars Lane, Hampstead Heath or Marlborough Avenue, or pubs like The Miners' Arms or King Charles Head.

How is it possible to look over a vista of green fields and small, mining villages and think of a Tumulus, Stone Circles and a Standing Stone. The Norman Church dominates the village of Llannon, it must have been built very close to the field where Non, the mother of St. David had a favourite resting place. The village has consisted of scattered farms and only recently there has been some bungalow's and houses built. It is a strange mixture for any congregation, I have heard the Vicar say . . . old established families and their children and another type of inhabitant, newcomers who live in the newly built houses which have filled the green fields around the Church, a group which are more affluent and are not perhaps as ready to become part of the history of their new environment. Perhaps they have not yet realised the long history connected with their new home.

One road leads to a mountain, Sylen. At the end of the last century there was one period of violence when people came from a wide area to meet and plan their rebellion against the ruthless landowners, these were Rebecca's people. Rebecca's Daughters with trousers under their skirts and their ruddy faces rubbed with honest dirt to disguise harder masculine lines. They rode from farm to farm on tough Welsh ponies to break down the toll gates where they had to pay their money just to pass. Desperation led to these measures, punishment a permanent exile to Australia. They burnt down the barriers to their lives and independence. In my house I have picture of one meeting on Sylen.

The empty mountain where once the oppressed farm people made their plans. The place has atmosphere composed from a history of thousands of years. Before the church was built and afterwards, different generations had different problems.

Who would think that the old Farm Marchoglwyn, Knight of The Bush, housed a knight who trained an army (although I have not yet discovered on whose side that army was meant to fight) on the fields where men grazed their cattle long after the Neolithic astronomers, before the Church in the dark grove of Llannon was built. Who could imagine the terrible rites between the circle of oak trees, some carved in those pre-historic shapes and primitive totems? Where was the pool where the treasures were thrown . . . Ffynnon Non?

There are the established geographical, concerning the boundaries There is a valley which is between heights. On a map one is able to see how the parish boundaries are marked by the Llangyndeyrn Mountain on the west and how Mynydd Sylen and Mynydd Mawr guarded the Gwendraeth Valley which flows down towards Kidwelly. The parish is composed of a close community and after a while I was to appreciate the comment as much as my neighbours that all bad weather came from Swansea. Our world was exposed but sheltered . . . on the whole. The hills and river bed gave a clue regarding ancient forces which had created a varied and interesting landscape.

There was the Gwendraeth Fach with its rich red sandstone soil but around Llannon itself, the centre of the area the soil was heavy and full of clay. Blue mud I have heard it called. The features were formed over millions of years by ice flows and water flows plus the movement of the earth's crust. Under such hard layers it is not surprising that there were coal seams found of really good quality. Anthracite, so pure that it could be held in a hand and not a mark of dust could be seen and it cut like a diamond. From research among the notes from a manuscript by Noel Gibbard it has been established that the megalithic builders came to Britain from the Iberian and Brittany seaboards. And there are three types of monuments which remain as evidence to this fact. There are chamber tombs, stone circles and a standing stone. The Church itself has its own history although nothing is known about its actual building. I had some information about the connection with certain churches with the prefix Llan that they were usually created on a site where there had been a more ancient form of worship. Llan-nonn, therefore, is its proper name. A living tradition is the story about Steddfa, a farm which should have the proper name of Eisteddfa Nonn and there was an old settle in the fields, Nonn's favourite resting place. A farm like Ciddewi connects us with the tradition of the Saint himself. All of this makes me certain that I was meant to write about this. A few weeks ago on a lovely evening in May, I was talking to my friends outside our house and I was asking questions regarding Llannon. This was because two of them lived there and the other friend had a great-aunt who still farmed in the area. One of my friends actually lived in a restored portion of Steddfa Farm, another was able to tell me several stories about the village and the third friend could tell of some items of historical value were discovered in one of the fields belonging to her aunt. One ride from here to the top of the mountain and the farm Ynysteddfa still stands with its windows looking across the valley and towards Cornwall on the other side – maybe towards her 'Cathedral of the Moors', Altarnun.

I had some items of importance myself which I had been given about twenty-five years ago which provided real proof of the Tumulus and the Standing Stone. In fact I had seen these features with my own eyes. I shall not forget the way one surface of that stone was plastered with flies . . . as if they had found refuge there on a very long flight. It was exactly what I wanted to connect the flora and fauna of Gwaunydd Cochion with a centre of Druidism which I felt certain had once been the main purpose of Llannon.

Llannon therefore, is its proper name Llannon and the Druid Connection. The church is named after the mother of St. David, St. Non and is an representation of the advent of Christianity in the area. What layers of our history lie behind this significant factor are in centuries, even millenniums of human development. We might use as another marker the chamber tombs, stone circles and a Standing Stone which I have seen for myself, although it is not reached the realms of curiosity and wonderment for which other regions might have strived.

The distant use of this land is veiled in mystery. From the network of tribes bound in Druidism there is no written evidence. Perhaps an isolated comment by Julius Caesar who give the opinion of a wartime invader faced with the resistance of a country under threat. His military mind mentions the fighting organisation in which the leaders directed without being involved in danger. He writes also, with horror that seems more genuine that the need to stir up disgust and a righteous desire to suppress, of the motives, almost understandable, of the principle 'death to repay deaths' which had been sustained by the Ancient Britains, a difference being in the case of Druidism, these killings are more than a natural revenge for a people but an act to appease their own gods. He tells of the role of the priests who do not take part in the routines themselves but are immune, as if they are not subject to a national call up. The extension of an 'eye for an eye' principle leads to a mass sacrifce of captured enemies, their enemies, their own criminals and many ordinary people for good measure. The chosen victims are crowded into a huge wicker-made giant made from the branches taken from their woodlands, arms, legs, thighs, body are filled with humans and the whole is then set alight to blaze in a monumental sacrifice. Because their power, it is said that the Romans made it their business to kill all the leaders. The void was established.

Another reason for the cloak to make more mysterious their era, results from the fact that the powerful priests alone had the right and ability to record their period in history: their rules, achievements; their poetry and knowledge gained from the natural world, of plants and their uses, a veritable material medica; knowledge of the stars, mathematical studies which are proved by their knowledge of direction and their understanding of the occult, their reading of the future, the entrails of an slaughtered animal is an example. Mystery enhanced by the convention of oral communication, not valuable when most of the scholars had been killed.

What gives a hint of the reality is the indisputable evidence of their inhabiting the sites of established holy places, their worship in the woodlands, after they had left the places of the Beaker People, the Stonehenge. In the woodlands there were their icons of carved oaks and wells and the typical lay out of a central point surrounded by fields and farmlands; there would always be the Well and the deep grove which would be their centre of worship, and their utter dependence of the naturals world, stars and sun, plants and animals.

Before the Church and after the Neolithic period. But there were no trees, especially no large oak trees to form the type of grove I wanted to imagine. It was strange that the one piece of evidence was found amongst the notes by the same historian, 'In 1748 the greatest number of trees growing in the churchyard were lately cut down and sold away.' There, now the picture was complete. According to Celtic traditions oral history referred to the passing of knowledge from one generation to the next, there would be nothing would be in writing, only shapes of stones and trees and the carving of a river across land, but according to witnesses at the time, the pagan rites which took place were sufficient to shock even the Roman armies. References are bound to be taken from isolated sources. Perhaps reports from Roman Generals when they invaded the Celtic regions and, in spite of their own brutal record, were shocked by the scenes of worship in these dark, sacred groves.

A paragraph taken from Nora Chadwick's *The Celts* is an example . . . 'A grove there, was untouched by man's hands from ancient times, whose interlacing boughs enclosed a space of darkness and cold shade, and banished the sunlight above. No rural Pan dwelt there, nor Silvanus, ruler of the woods, no nymphs, but gods were worshipped with savage rites, the altars were heaped with hideous offerings, and every tree was sprinkled with human gore. On these boughs, if antiquity, reverential of the gods, deserved any credit, birds feared to perch; in these coverts wild beasts would not lie down, no wind ever bore down upon that wood, nor thunderbolt hurled from black clouds; the trees even when they spread their leaves to a breeze, rustled among themselves. Water also fell there in abundance from dark springs. The images of Gods, grim and rude, were uncouth blocks formed of felled tree trunks.' I could say more, but it ends with a note that even the priests were nervous.

* * *

The legacy of this Pagan scene is linked to dark woodland surrounded by oak trees and rough carved figures from these mighty oaks which formed circles for rituals. Sacrifices . . . wicker cages filled with victims; blood on rude altars, entrails on trees and deep pools where treasures were lowered. The chosen highlight might be the sacrifice of the purest maiden. The Queen of the May. The pool is hidden now, maybe in the grounds of the Church or a nearby field, perhaps close to where Nonn sat and dreamt her young thoughts. In Llanstephan a similar place is still used for visitors to throw their coins and make wishes. At Gwaunydd Cochion, a well was used more recently for baptisms. In the villages the tradition is still strong when the Queen is chosen for the carnivals. Gaiety and flowers, not exactly going out to the country to bring in the May, but ceremony and decorated floats and flowers. Sinister connotations have been long forgotten the fact that the garlands of flowers on the float, cleaned of its everyday work evidence, which could be anything from coal dust to straw bales, would be the preparation of a stage prior to the sacrifice. The trees, a sacred oak; the power of the priests; use of narcotic herbs and understanding besides the worship of nature.

A fleeting memory of a story about a visit to Belsen or Austwitch where no birds could sing.

It is such a relief to bring the history of the Church to more modern times and to hear some of the recent life in the parish. Even the true story which seems ridiculous when recounted many years after, but at the time would be merely a matter of commonsense, the tale of an elephant which was housed in the Church overnight (the circus came to Llannon with regularity in those days) which ate all its hay and, for afters, devoured the candles. Great confusion ensued when the keeper, in the dark, could not locate it. Remember there was no light . . . the elephant had seen to that.

It is good to think of weddings, christenings and funerals and normal village life, even the carnivals.

Christianity took over with political tact so that for a while the new religion must have blended without absolute rejection. We had Christmas with Holly and the Mistletoe. Red berries and there were silver coins in the Holy Wells in Cornwall which were mostly named from the saints. Tags of clothing or personal items blew in the breeze on trees around a sacred church when Christianity came into its own. Llan; a church in a grove; my area around Llannon with all the physical features. There might be an old tree with a thick root which twines around it as if it is a serpent; old roots and ivy which the emphasis on the Triad is an essential Celtic twining and has the same intricate pattern.

Gwaunydd Cochion is a stretch of purple Moorgrass which lies in front of the local hospital and Tumble and Cross Hands became the places where the miners had their houses built.

When I drove to the place where I was to work in Great Mountain Colliery, so many years ago, there were other mountains, large conical tips which looked black and covered in scrub and I could never have imagined how I was to love the place. Llannon was set just off the main Llanelli Road on the way to Hendy. The Norman Church really was Llannon and a friend of ours who was a local grave digger in the churchyard often told us how the soil there was heavy and full of clay. 'Blue mud' explained over and over again, and would tell us how difficult it was to work.

My task in the next few pages is to take from a list of plants which was the official list of plants which grew in the stretch of purple moorgrass in front of the hospital, which is very close to Llannon, and see which ones would have been used by the Druids. Subsequently . . .

by the Physicians of the Myddfai. There was a connection. As the crow flies for example and there was a marriage between one distinguished family in Llannon to a member of the family from Middleton Hall which is in the fertile area around the Tawe.

In a book by David Conway, *The Magic of Herbs*, there is a list of the seven sacred herbs of the Druids. All must have grown in the area.

Learning from Animals

This should read caring for animals and watching also listening to practical advice from those who have handled all kinds of animals for years.

Some things are indispensable. Firm bandages, liniments, antiseptics which must be in quite large quantities and large pads of cotton wool or in the modern world boxes of tissues.

I have spoken about the properties of Camphorated Oil and Vick and the benefit of a good liniment when applied. This is where experience of animals and appreciation of the treatment is counts, maybe it is the substance being used, but confidence in oneself and in the animal is important, even if the poor beast has to be tied down, although a soothing voice and care makes this almost always unnecessary. The cupboard with tiny bottles of this and that is to be confined to the bathroom, space is essential. Space to keep large quantities of whatever has to be always on hand and space for the animal . . . space to enable the handler to jump out of the way. There was one occasion, when the Vet who was working in a stable where the animal to be treated was too close to the others, said, 'There's too much traffic in here.'

Some people believe that the stronger concoctions made to penetrate the fur or hair of an animal brings more relief to themselves. One recipe which stands out because (a) it is different and (b) because it contains the universal cure which was the source of all that is good in past recipes, it is just another example of the value of the Elderflower tree.

To Make Elder Ointment:

Take a pint glass and fill it with elder blossom pickt clean from ye Stem, and then pour in some of ye best meat oyle, and fill ye glass and lett it stand against a sunny window for a fortnight, and so keep it for use. 'Tis good for a strain or ach or bruise, use it cold by chafe it in by ye fire. Ye flowers must not be strained offe. 1727.

This ancient recipe does not appear to be made according to strict hygienic rules. It seems to relate to the all cure application of Goose Grease which is used with faith by many modern countrymen. The following recipe illustrates how Elder Oil is used for other conditions. Once again this proves how important for all creatures is that Elderflower tree at the edge of the yard. At this moment as we near autumn

I know I shall see the branches of my tree sway up and down as very plump pigeons arrive to eat the berries. One observation I feel I could make is how different the wood pigeons look from the thousands which inhabit the buildings in the towns.

Elder Oil, for cuts, burns and scalds. Pick elderflowers. Tie down in a very large jam jar or sweet bottle with wide top. Place in the *sun*. When all oil has oozed out strain into bottle. Will keep for years. Smarts, but heals. Rub on gently. Although this last advice does not say what makes the oil, or what is meant to top it up, which is the kind of thing which happens in 'things which are passed on' I have looked at another remedy for deep burns or scalds which uses Elder and this one mentions to mix the inner rind of elder with fresh butter. It adds, to bind this paste on with a rag and plunge the part into cold water. All these remedies which have been handed down through decades make one significant point which we must remember, that is that we have learnt the importance of cleanliness and sterilisation and how quickly bacteria reproduce in the situations mentioned in those old adages, it is best to use them for comparison unless they make sense.

THE IMPORTANCE OF LINIMENTS

For the moment I shall concentrate on liniments because I have depended on them so often. Most of them have been tried and tested personally. They have been used so often and if my horses could speak I am sure they would swear on their beneficial effects, as do many sportsmen who rub Wintergreen or Lin Meth Sal into their strains and bruises after a match.

Minor ailments and daily accidents are part of the routine when one has to care for animals. There is real desperation if an animal is ill or injured badly enough to phone the vet. Usually there is a crisis, perhaps it happens in a field when one is out of reach of the telephone. These days the mobile 'phone is a blessing. An animal is not able to explain symptoms and sometimes is not even able to be left . . . the need for treatment is immediate. There is the possibility that the animal develops an illness during the night and even with the best stable or food in the world it needs 'The eye of the master' constantly. It is not possible to gain a history to make a diagnoses when there is no evidence and no explanation. I read a book once by Henry Blake, *Talking To Animals*; there was so much in that book which helped me when I was looking after a group of Welsh cobs in some land I had rented in Pontyates. I learnt the difference in their calls and behavioural patterns which made life easier for them and myself. One subject Henry Blake was interested in and had studied was Extra-sensory Perception which, very briefly, means having knowledge of needs and feelings between two animals when there is a distance between them. The animals must have a close relationship and need not be the same type. It might be two mares, a gelding and a mare, two companions who graze together or the horse and owner. This subject was studied and in short, means that when one of the creatures is in trouble, somehow the partner in the relationship will know.

Another factor is trust has to exist between the animal and the person who cares for it, trust plus a little faith in whatever medical substance is at hand before things can return to normal. One mare has a condition which I have to treat each day throughout the season. She has a very fine skin which flinches at the slightest brush of an insect. A lot of horses suffer from Sweet Itch which comes in the spring and the autumn, this has various causes, midges obviously, but certain herbs cause an allergy, In Jan's case she is also allergic to the sun. Each day I mix my lotions and potions and wait for the quiet moment in the stable when I can treat her. It was painful, the standard treatment given by the Veterinary Practice did not suit her and made all attempts to apply remedies difficult. This was a case when it was essential to obtain trust and now, instead of the flinching, backing away and that pathetic shivering of the skin, I am able to approach her with confidence, rub more surely and she even has a little doze when I treat her. During the past few years she has learnt this fact for herself and whenever the sun is too fierce she runs into the comparative darkness of a stable. I have learnt to keep the stable door open for her.

When she is in the middle of summer the condition becomes more general, her eyes are sunken and she shelters as much as she is able. These are the times when she will not let anyone touch but, as has been explained, I have managed to get the matter under control. Lately, in America there is a long lasting drug to be injected which will give prolonged relief from allergy, hay fever especially. It is not available here but sometime, in the future I shall be able to try it.

Animal owners have favourite remedies which have been proven by other people and passed on through hearsay. They might be discovered by a desperate experiment as in one of the above circumstances before help arrives or before the actual remedy is discovered. I have listed some of mine and there are many more. An incident or remark made at the time fixes it in memory. My mare had an infected rash under the fringe on her forehead. Ordinary application of antiseptics kept it dry but did not cure it. It affected her and her rubbing against any non-sterile object which happened to be at hand made it worse. I had tried most of the ointments which were available. One lotion which was very much in vogue was recommended so constantly that I tried it and the rash, so far under control became virulent. I cleared all trace of this from her head. A niece of mine, quite out of the blue told me her daughter had something similar and she had used almond oil. This was for the kitchen I thought, but I tried it and the rash cleared immediately. I do not know why.

Wintergreen, this is described as a small creeping evergreen plant which grows 5-6″ high under such shrubs as Kalmia's and Rhododendrons. The oil from the leaves is the official source, although it is possible the whole plant may be used. It contains 99% Methyl Salicylate and only ·3 of a hydrocarbon, Gaul herilene and secondary aldehyde or Ketone makes up the whole. This little part gives it that unmistakable smell. The leaves have to be steeped for over twelve hours for the oil to develop sufficiently for extraction. Native North Wintergreen is said to be applied via a cloth soaked with the oil to relieve pain in joints. As always in these remedies whether they are herbal or not, use with caution. It contains analgesic and astringent properties; it is a diuretic and stimulant. The leaves are used for a headache. It is well to mention that in most cases the cure is more effective because of the accompanying massage of the hands plus the soothing voice.

One memory which is powerful, perhaps I should have mentioned it in the childhood chapter, is of coming home at dinner time and finding my mother with a severe headache. I was sent to Timothy White's to get a Menthol Rub. For some reason there was not one in the house which was unusual because was, her considered, infallible remedy. I have used it myself with caution, it had an immediate effect when rubbed across the forehead, but it was wise to close the eyes because the fumes released were powerful.

Fiery Jack is the name for a strong liniment which sounds as if it is based on one of the above recipes; there was a chemist is Carmarthen who mixed his own brand of liniment for horses and this was used by my husband who said the other brand names were ineffectual. It was important to have a bottle in the stable. Sometimes when it was possible by feeling down the leg or part affected, to touch the exact centre of pain, the rubbing (away from the heart) brought relief very quickly to the animal. Modern vets and people who care for horses know that sometimes a constant application of cold water brings ease. This makes one realise how effective an ice-pack is to an athlete who is in trouble.

Wintergreen is a constituent in an effective herbal inhalant which is available in pharmacies and health shops. I do suffer from catarrh and this can be best described as being a miserable condition without being life threatening. At the beginning of summer, the pollen count might make things a little worse and this year I tried the above remedy. It was relieving and comforting and impressed me so much that I read the list of contents which were as follows: Cajuput Oil, Eucalyptus Oil, Juniper Berry Oil, Clove Oil, Menthol, Peppermint and Wintergreen. All of those are familiar but the one which interested me most was Cajuput Oil from the Tea Tree. This, I have mentioned before in my treatment of animals section and lately it has become more well known, being included in shampoos and body lotions. I have used it in its purest oil form and when I soak the mane or sponge over the body of my mare with a troublesome skin condition I always add a few drops. It is pleasing to know that a remedy has found to be effective and also to prove the benefit of favourite herbs.

I shall now tell the story which will prove how Vick brought about a dramatic recovery in a very lovely foal I had once . . . Morgelyn. I shall have to begin with Rhoswyn, the mare and mother. This is a story which depends on character.

Rhoswyn was a beautiful filly when we bought her from a friend. She is now almost thirty, which is quite old, even for the Welsh cob breed, but unlike humans, she is even more lovely in old age. She is a bay and this is where I would differ from traditional descriptions of colours. A chestnut in equine terms is a reddish, ginger colour, but to me Rhoswyn's coat which is the exact colour of a chestnut shell, burnished to perfection, as we see them piled in the shelves at Christmas, is a much better image. She is just about fourteen hands high and has the proportions of any successful model. Her movements, although now dignified and definite, have always been those of a natural dressage performer. In all this beauty the point which has made her outstanding is the thick, free falling mane which flies backwards like a black wing when she trots or canters towards you. If I thought to own a prize was more important than keeping my mare out of the world of stress and competition, Rhoswyn would have won a range of rosettes. Friends have begged me to allow them to show her. During these conversations, Rhoswyn stands by my side, confident and assured that she will remain serene and safe in her own surroundings.

One of the contents in an animal's first-aid cupboard would be a supply of Comfrey. Now it is obtainable in neat little pots or if it is a lotion in bottles. Perhaps at one time it was taken internally according to some of the old books and the ability it had to cure all kinds of ailments inside, but in its natural state it could be used as a poultice.

The plant itself is a member of the Borage or Forget-me-not tribe. In fact a young plant which has not developed looks very much like a primrose when not in flower. A more intent inspection will show that the leaves have a rougher and a hairy appearance, and it is possible to see that they are destined to grow in a longer and oval shape. It is in bloom throughout the greater part of the Summer. It has been used as a fodder plant in Eastern Europe and has the reputation of being a worthy green food because it contains a lot of flesh forming substances. This reputation might be gained through its habit of healing and preventative properties. It has been used as a preventative and even as a curative of foot and mouth disease. I was first introduced to it by an elderly blacksmith and his opinion has been seconded by almost everyone who ha anything to do with animals or healing. When health shops widened their market appeal, it was easily available here but until then, this kind of commodity was found in horse fairs or game fairs. I suppose that is one reason for the word of mouth method of passing on personal knowledge. It was not long ago when I saw I television film about long sea journeys when the ship's surgeon was setting up his supply of needs for the journey and a large bunch of Comfrey leaves were packed into his cabin. The name Knitbone seems to give it sufficient recommendation. Ship's surgeons knew that the powdered root, if dissolved in water to a mucilage (a sticky consistency) will hasten the callus of bones under repair and will control haemorrhage.

I have friends who keep horses who have used it as a poultice. Even when the wound has had dangerous foreign bodies to complicate it, i.e. gravel, dirt, even bits of stitches left after an operation or splinters of a broken bone.

There are always other animals I have treated . . . in the past they have been brought to me by neighbours. Sometimes my own Welsh cobs have been involved. Once or twice I have willed them to relax and be almost asleep when (to them) danger seems to threaten.

One example was the first visit of a blacksmith to the foals, even though they were with their mares and sometimes the mother tries to reassure them in her own way, I knew this would be quite an ordeal for them. I maneuvered each pair into a stable and set about calming them prior to the arrival of Mark, the blacksmith. The mares were almost sleeping on their feet and the foals lying in the straw. Victoria and Sarah, two children from a neighbouring farm who had each adopted one of the foals, arrived to watch this important trimming of their feet. They arrived with too much energy and the fact they had both been given one of those whirling rattling gadgets usually seen on a football field added to the disruption.

It is good to work well with the blacksmith. They have such a store of knowledge and apart from hearing a few good stories, they are able to teach many lessons. At times owner and blacksmith have to work with each other. One example is when Holly, a roan gelding, had a badly bruised foot. In the equine world this means a condition which is more painful than our idea of a bruise, it is an area on the painful surface of the hoof which has to be paired away, Holly could not put this foot on the ground after treatment and we were one field's distance from the stable. I placed a pad of Glycerine and Icthammol under the foot and drew one of my stockings over this to keep it in place. He was able to walk. I know the link is tenuous but Thyme is the plant of origin in this case. What matters in all these cases is the trust given by an animal. I have said to many animals, dogs, horses, goats – even Margot – a lovely Aberdeen Angus, when they are hesitant and fail to walk where I have indicated or eaten something which makes them dubious, 'Trust me'. They respond, almost without fail. I do not know why, it is like certain other words, 'Whoa' and 'Steady' words that transcend language and beast.

Another tenuous link. In this case it is beer and the hop. Where there is a case of colic which is due to a twist in the alimentary canal, it was said that a warm drink of beer would straighten out the bend and relieve the symptoms. I had heard of this previously but I could not rely on my memory. I checked with Mr. Lyn Evans, who was a Veterinary Surgeon, with whom I had worked so many times when my horses were ill. He told me it was quite true in past years. The farmers might just pour down a bottle of the drink but to be more professional, the Vets would use a funnel and a rubber tubing. Now the treatment is quite different. The endless walking up and down which was done to take the animals mind of his pain and to prevent him lying down has been improved, there is now an injection which relaxes the muscles. I tried to find something about the hop which might have made it significant . . . only one thing from Culpepper seemed to have a connection, that 'Hops loosens the belly and provoketh urine.' It could be the soothing warmth of the drink. Faith and trust seems to add an extra dimension to which ever cure is brought into use and this includes the modern drugs. It has to be given with confidence and accompanied by care. Care counts as love. Psychology is a strange concept if considered in relation to animals. Humans unfamiliar in this relationship are bound to think those who would apply semi-intellectual approach are sentimental idiots.

It is the opposite. Once again trust must be established and for this and any method capable of creating a bond is useful. For once I see sense in that caption, 'Trust rules OK'. Right from the beginning it will make an animal calm and interested. If the procedure is pleasant, i.e. getting the mouth to accept something to promote sucking or chewing; a caress which gives pleasure; a calm approach with unthreatening bodily movements, this might even mean a clever method of appearing to retreat when making an advance. For myself the important principle is to think a positive way forward and dismiss any personal anxiety, fear or even anguish. On one occasion when I had to take my beloved Genna, my golden labrador, to the Vet to be put down, I gave myself the ultimate test. Genna went with confidence and even wagging her tail, to her fate

I forced every negative thought from my mind, refusing to talk to anyone and concentrating on any good moment we had shared together. It was worth it for Genna. I know she did not sense anything. My hands were giving out my love as she was on the table. I felt a slight change in the hairs on the coat, after about, and this is utterly true, only three seconds. I looked into the Vet's eye and said, 'I think it is taking effect.' She answered, 'Yes . . . she's gone.'

Afterwards, I returned to the car park, the empty collar and lead in my hand.

Such love might help an animal to chew, one ash leaf, maybe two . . . three. I take a small spray in and my goat who has been given up as a hopeless case, is looking almost with interest as I enter. Touching and tenderness are not mentioned in medical, veterinary or herbal books, but never omit this ingredient.

I like goats. They fascinate me because of their individuality. People who have looked after goats will know of their habit of giving up too easily, they lack the will to survive. It is almost as if they will lie down and die whenever they are depressed. A positive quality is they have intelligence . . . they think. I know this is admirable but when they outthink their owners it makes things awkward.

A little nanny goat of mine responded to the method I described above, tempting, caressing, causing the first mouth movements until she ate with relish some of her favourite food . . . leaves from the Ash trees.

That was another thing which made me enjoy having goats, the gathering of branches for their overnight food sacks.

Next to trust or perhaps before trust I would put observation on the list of qualities suitable for a hinds man.

Careful watch goes without saying. Sometimes the putting two and two together is not easy. I came home once and looked in the opposite field and saw Holly, my roan gelding and Honey, my sturdy mare, grazing. They looked contented. Not very long afterwards I looked a second time and saw that Honey still had a length of fern in her mouth. This made me wonder. The fern remained and by this time Holly was grazing a little distance from his companion. I went in and examined Honey's mouth and realised she was unable to chew. I called the Vet and this was the start of a long illness. For weeks I fed Honey on things she could just about draw into her mouth, Bran with apples or carrots or any soft mash. She wanted to graze and each day went out into the field, her mouth hovering over the luscious grass which is the staple diet of the equine. She could not move her jaws to chew. Gradually, she lost weight and on the day I lifted my hand to catch hold of her head collar and saw her head withdraw as if the pain was too much to contemplate. I thought I would have to ask the Vet who had been in close touch all the while to put her down.

He was coming on the Monday. On the Sunday night I came in after giving Honey her last feed and a bit of extra attention and realised my hand had an unpleasant smell of pus, in spite of washing thoroughly. I washed my hands again to be certain and there was no improvement. I went out to the stable with a pad and placed this under Honey's jaw and something had broken. I bathed it well, repeated this in the morning and put her out in front of the house to see what happened. She was able to graze . . . with relish. Grass the most important food for all herbivores. I phoned the Vet, Mr. Clive Adams. He was as pleased as I was. 'I will come over just to see her,' he said. He did. Honey recovered.

It is so obvious perhaps, but I have not mentioned how different animals have their own characteristics and react according to their own disposition. This is especially the case in our pets, with me, as I have spent many years with them, in the case of Welsh cobs. I make the difference because the Welsh breed is entirely separate. I shall never forget my first sight of one at Llanybyther Market. It was neither a horse nor a pony. It happened to be a stallion because it was the occasion in the year when the best of the stallions from the famous Stud Farms of Cardiganshire are brought to be seen by the owners of mares who intend to improve their own stock and perpetuate the ancient lines. Here everyone who is around appears knowledgeable and at one time I felt I knew enough to be able to take part in the ensuing conversations. I have a book written by Dr. Wynne Davies, *Welsh Ponies and Cobs* (published by J. A. Allen), that I would not part with for the world. From that first sight I have never considered any other animal which could compare, except maybe, a wonderful Arab from the Arabian Nights. The book gives an invaluable insight into the breeding of the Welsh cob, especially in Cardiganshire.

Honey was the first Welsh cob we bought. As a character, she was exactly like the letters in lights which advertised a film in London in the forties . . . I forget the name of the film and the actress but the caption said 'MEAN . . . MOODY . . . AND MAGNIFICENT'. She depended on me so much, the above anecdote will explain that. She had several difficult foalings and when I first bought her she needed some extra care. She was an honest mare, in her way. She would never try to throw you and if you were on her back she was amenable and very comfortable. I used to take my Christmas cards around on her; take bottles of fruit juice and food to the men and girls working on the hay harvest. She always knew if there was a child on her back and in her old age, she was a favourite with them. Her eyes glowed with pleasure when they visited her and she was as gentle as a teddy bear. I think she knew they meant short rides and not very much weight . . . plus a few treats like Polo Mints and Carrots.

In the beginning I thought it would be good to have a foal from her. Because I believed in the purity in the water on the top of Sylen and the widespread growth of herbs which grew there, that is where she grazed. I was sure I was right. M. David Jones, Disgwylfa, agreed with me. Each day I would go up with a bucket of feed and a little pan for her companion. We had a routine. I would hide Honey's bucket amongst the furze and go into the field. Honey would go out and search for her bucket as I stayed with and fed Silva. When Honey had finished, she would return to her field and her companion. I would talk to them for a while and they would resume their grazing. As I write this I have a mental picture of some of the many books written by expert herbalists that I have been reading. All these books, especially the weightier volumes, among which I would give most credit to *A Modern Herbal* by Mrs. M. Grieve, contain so much knowledge. Some of this knowledge has been practiced for thousands of years and by people we have underestimated, and I realise how valuable are so many of the common plants in the pastures grazed by our animals. Everything which is essential is within their spheres. And we sometimes resort to supplementary vitamins.

Honey had several difficult foalings. I remember the longing in her eyes once when she lost her foal and saw Rhoswyn with Morgelyn for the first time. Of course, Rhoswyn would not allow her to come near, but Honey grazed as close as she dared until the ban was lifted. Therefore, the summer I shall always call my golden summer was when my three mares had foals of equal beauty. Honey with Isolde, Kelynen with Delen and Rhoswyn with Tamara. Of the three mares, Honey was the one I watched as she trained her foal to jump over a large ditch which was in the middle of the field.

Two plants I must mention here, one is the Marigold. There are many things associated with this bright summer blossom that are taken for granted. It has been advocated by artistic cooks to make salads more decorative; I mentioned the practice of growing one little marigold plant in the corner of the greenhouse. I have done it this season and it has made my humble glass shelter for those three or four tomato plants and a cucumber look brilliant. It grows here safe from slugs which have always appreciated it. One other touch of colour comes from the Courgette plant. Other uses associated with the Marigold, and I used this so often without realising what I was doing because it was sold under the name of Calendula, is the shampoo which repels insects and an ointment which has extra healing powers. The shampoo was very effective when I shampooed the mane of Jan, who has so many allergies. The ointment healed many small sores, even the scrapes on my arm which were frequent when Kelly, my sheepdog, was young and exuberant.

As I write this I realise just how important these moments of caring for animals are. I can see Honey now in her winter field, trotting down from the top shelter (with the others following) through the snow, her head bent downwards and sideways as she avoided the stinging of the flakes in her eyes. She did live to a ripe old age and I had her right to the end.

I have had animals which, as they say in their horsy jargon, 'Do not carry much condition.' This means, at times that they are as thin as rakes; their coat is staring; they are under stress and need much love and attention. Not my fault! This is not a case of 'she would say that, wouldn't she' but the loss of condition might be due to illness, malnutrition before I bought it, stress and sometimes because the animal is 'not a good doer.'

Bran (Boiling water poured on 2 lbs. Bran), the bucket left as the water steamed through the grain and created the most wholesome of smells, (I am beginning to sound like Culpepper). To make this mixture more delectable I would add grated carrot or apple!

As I write I am thinking of opening my own equine restaurant on the River Thames.

I have noticed at times when riding and there is a chance to rest, an older horse will chew a few leaves of Ivy. Experienced friends have told me that this happens when, perhaps due to an instinctive need, which may be an underlying chest trouble. I looked into the properties of Ivy to see what was the connection.

In Jean Palaiseul's book, *Grandmother's Secrets*, I read Ivy may be used for inflammatory conditions such as cellulitis and rheumatism sciatica and swellings when there is heat in them. Another advantage is that it is a strong plant, abundant and always green which grows around us for all seasons. It needs only a simple application, fresh leaves either chopped or applied to the skin or made into poultices, in this case two handfuls, finely chopped and mixed with four ounces of Bran with hot water. This may be dismissed as merely an application of heat but there is a description of another form of first aid when, 'if a cock was inured in a cockfight, especially the eye, the owner would chew some Ground Ivy and spit into the wounded bird's eye.'

This does suggest that this is something that has a beneficial effect on the tissues.

For a bad toothache, 20 grammes of Ivy leaves boiled in a glass of red wine, a pinch of coarse salt and ½ glass of vinegar; rinse around with this mixture and it will help the pain. Even in the medical centre we relied on an application of Oil of Cloves, which seemed to numb the area where the pain was.

Sometimes the cure is kept secret. This was the case when a friend could not get her mare to walk because of an injury to the foot. She was a long way from home. Two gypsies came along and looked at the foot; they then gathered a plant from the hedge and pounded it with a stone. They applied it and the foot was cured in a short while . . .

able to walk. My friend and the gypsies chatted as they waited and she was anxious to know what was the mixture. They would not tell her. All she knew was that it was red. I remember in hospital in the old days we had a lotion that is not used these days, probably forgotten with all the new drugs and discoveries at hand. It was Lotia Rubra. When I looked up Madder, in one book it was listed with the Bedstraw family, Rubiaceae along with Cleavers and Blue Woodruff, in Mrs. M. Grieve's book there was much more about the plant which has some commercial use and the colour red is mentioned (after treatment). This is one case when guessing is not good enough and the mystery remains.

This is my treatment. It begins as always with care to establish trust. My initial wash was with a simple saline solution. In case it might have had a fungal origin I sponge her with Permanganate of Potash. In this case I use my experience of working with miners when Athletes' Foot was a common condition and the first treatment was a foot bath with this solution. I do this once or twice a day. Then, with great care I apply a special concoction made up of pure Olive Oil with drops of Lavender, Camomile and Tea Tree (essential oils) mixed in a small container. I choose the worst spots for this stage of treatment; if one spot is very raw, I apply Camomile on its own or Calendula (Marigold) in an ointment form. I have found this recommended in other spheres. As I work with the mare she relaxes.

At one time I had to tie her and go through a ritual before I could get her halter on. This meant I stood in my corner as she backed into hers and, never chasing her, I waited until she came towards me and often, ducked her head into the outstretched halter. Once she was used to the treatment she did not flinch even when I came to the sore spots and I could rub the oil quite firmly into these places. I found Almond Oil useful for an area under the fringe of her mane which was made worse through constant rubbing against woodwork.

Once I had her in the stable and tied her, a ritual which was essential in her case. She would back into her own corner of the stable and I would stay in mine (near the door) until she decided to come to me and place her head almost in the head collar on her own accord. I never chased her because that would be bad equine psychology. She did not flinch when it was time to touch the sore spots and soon I was able to rub the mixture quite firmly into the area. Under the fringe of her mane there was even another condition which was more irritable. This was a scaly condition which must have come after her rubbing her head against a post. I cured this, still having to cope with her resistance because it was so sore, with the use of Almond Oil. I had the same result. The scales disappeared and I was able to almost scrub the patch. I always began my treatment always with the sponge all over with Permanganate of Potash. This treatment was continued until the colder weather when she was her old self again. By this time only rough spots in her coat would show where the sores had been. In winter her coat shines and she is a picture of health.

Cobwebs, Cabbage and Cannabis

At times a remedy appears unlikely and on other occasions there is a substance which looks as if is bound to have healing properties

Imagine an early morning in September and there, between a few strands of a Chrysanthemum or on a thorny branch of a late Rose, there is a gossamer circle of a spider's web. No pattern could be more intricate and the drawing together of this fine lace seems to have a mystical connection with drawing together or healing.

The second very unlikely factor about this silken artistry is its connection with death, it is the trap to snare the prey for the rather ugly little monster who has eight legs and usually eight eyes.

No wonder they are so difficult to capture as they run across the floor just as one watches a television programme.

There are house spiders and our familiar garden spiders . . . I suppose the spiders who make their homes in a stable must be one or the other. In either case it is a predator. In this country we do not have the Black Widow, the Tarantula, or the Zebra spider which stalks its prey or the Bird-eating spider whose body is about 2-4 in long and a leg-span of 1 ft. The threads on which the spider swings and shapes to capture its fly or passing insect are formed from the spinnerets which are on the under surface of the abdomen.

No . . . it is not likely that we would take this masterpiece from its setting when blood is to be stanched.

Many years ago I must have heard that a spiders web was used in by old physicians and healers; it was one of those stories we forget, there is not often reason to remember it unless one lives in the country when there is more time to talk and often more incidents to relate.

A friend once told me about a mare who had received quite a deep wound in the shoulder muscle due to a violent contact with the protruding branch of a tree as she was galloping along a path in the woodland. The Vet was a distance away and would not be available for at least an hour and a half and the wound was bleeding. A farmer suggested plugging the wound with a cobweb; because several of the group nodded their heads at the suggestion and said that it was the best thing to do in the circumstance, this was the plan. The problem was that the stable in which the mare was being treated was newly white-washed and very hygienic. However, not very far away, there was a stable which had thick oak beams along the roof and was a place which was the summer retreat for generations of swallows. There were plenty of cobwebs in that roof. Two messengers were sent and alas, not an ethereal silken dressing, but a solid plug of a sticky brown substance was procured but stopped the bleeding with great success. The fluid which exudes from the spinnerets is viscid and hardens on exposure to form the silky threads. I should imagine the nearest a human might get to this intricate work is when a Master Chef spins a web of molten sugar threads to make a pattern over an exquisite desert. It must be admitted, even in our modern days when sterile conditions at home and in hospitals are of a high standard, the idea of using something of this substance might have merit in an emergency.

I look at a remedy which calls for cobwebs which I discovered in the book of *Cornish Recipes* published by the National Federation of Women's Institutes in 1930 (only 68 years ago). It is for the Ague, which is and, this is as far as I can understand, a general fever which is accompanied by a temperature, raised pulse and shivering. It says take six middling pills of cobwebs or apply to each wrist a plaster of treacle and soot. This item of wisdom comes from Devoran, a small village between Truro and Falmouth.

There are a few remedies which have an aura of witchcraft about them. I try to find a rational explanation in a few cases. Some I accept as an act of faith or, merely, just for fun. The above made me think. I could understand the rather sticky plug of a large cobweb being used as a styptic or to plug a wound which would otherwise be impossible to treat if out in the wilds somewhere. Modern scientists must have used the comparison with Alexander Fleming and his discovery of Penicillin which resulted from observation of an area clear of bacteria around the mouldy part of a piece of cheese. They might even have had this type of cobweb under a microscope to see its consistency. There was the sudden observation of Watts who realised the power of steam when he saw the lid of a kettle rising as the water boiled and wondered why they did not figure it out for themselves considering the number of times they had seen an apple drop. Yet . . . how can six pills made from cobwebs or a mixture of treacle and soot help in a condition known as Ague? The only thing I can think is that it is a substance sticky enough to make the pulse find beating a bit more difficult. I know, I know, this makes nonsense of the whole thing. I feel I could quote Culpepper here and say, although this is in a different context, (he is talking about hops) 'Mars owns the plant and then Dr. Reason tells you how it performs the actions.'

CABBAGE

A true description of this honest and lovely vegetable is given by Jean Palaiseul in her book *Grandmother's Secrets* she says it is 'The Doctor of the Poor' and this is followed by a number of the conditions it will alleviate if not cure absolutely. As a poultice or other application applied to affected area it is used for varicose ulcers, eczema, gangrene, burns wounds or contusions, carbuncles, rheumatic pains, neuralgia, migraines, sprains, wrenches, sciatica and lumbago. To make this poultice she advises to remove the raised central rib, pound the secondary side ribs and warm leaves with this on the stove or whichever heating facilities are available. A Savoy Cabbage is used when possible and it is easy to see why. The leaves of the Savoy are thick and full of goodness and greener than most plants. As a drink with suitable additives, i.e. lemon or maybe some of the mucilage from the Carrageen, it may be used to rid the bronchial system of phlegm in chest diseases.

Before we became used to the habit of having wine on the table and became too sophisticated, on Sundays it was my treat, and I mean treat, to drink a cup full of the water in which the cabbage was boiled. It was one of my perks. The rest always went to make the gravy.

I have mentioned my firend, Mr. David Jones, sadly long deceased, he was a true countryman. To him the ideas of motorways and tunnels built through good land was anathema. He walked his land Winter and Summer, matching all growth to the month of the year. When the temperature was high he would be on his hay-bob turning the whitening grass until it was 'made'. He knew by the feel of it and the sound of the rustle between his fingers when the time was right for bailing. In the heat he would wear his ancient straw hat, he could have been painted by Cezanne, and underneath this hat there would be a large cabbage leaf to 'stop him from having a headache,' he would explain. I have heard how the opposite applies. A hot cabbage leaf bound on to a swollen knee with a crepe bandage will give relief for a long while and even when there is pain in the breast it will form a soothing warm compress.

Last year I bought an Ornamental Cabbage. It was a beautiful thing, like a large green and red rose, perfect in every leaf. I set it in a prominent patch. When I went out to admire it in the morning, it had disappeared. There were tell tale trails of a silver thread and a few remnants of the last leaves to explain what had happened.

CANNABIS . . . HEMP

Hemp confuses also. The picture I have of hemp, brown and hanging under a shed somewhere in a hot climate; thick ropes or a swing bridge made of the roots of the plant high over a river which cuts through a ravine. It says that it is cultivated in most temperate countries. In several reference books 'hemp' is listed under Agrimony This makes Mother's Herby Beer Recipe much less than the innocent beverage we thought we drank.

In John Lust's *The Herb Book*, which I keep in my kitchen, there is a description of Cannabis. He says it is a herbaceous annual plant. It grows wild but can be (and often is illegally) cultivated in warm climates. It is found in many places in the United States. In this book it mentions the current use of the plant for its power to induce euphoria and the more serious effect of relieving pain, the plant has a reputation which I am certain is deserved as a medicinal agent. After this recommendation there follows a list of conditions which it is said to alleviate which includes, analgesic, hypnotic, anti-epileptic, anaesthetic (even antibiotic) conditions. It says plants grown in sandy soil are the most active medicinally. Cannabis has lost its beneficial aura because of its misuse in the modern drug culture. I have never smoked it. However, I attended lectures given by the Police when I was a Nursing Officer, which were given to enable us to recognize the smell, the appearance, the type of cigarette packet which seemed to be favoured by the 'users'. The lectures were given to prevent the spread of the habit which seemed to be taking a hold on the young people. The habit was spreading. We found it difficult to believe. I had a friend who was doing a course in Social Nursing in a rural area around Tregaron. We exchanged experiences and I realised then that her main problem was found amongst the teen-agers. It was not pneumoconiosis amongst miners but drug addiction amongst young people. The rural community was not immune from the foibles of town-dwellers. Note: Today . . . 30th June, 1998, there was a piece of interest pertaining to Cannabis on the radio, saying there was an increase in this practice in rural areas. Has it worsened or have they just discovered this fact?

Hemp works on the higher nerve centres. It can produce an exhilarating intoxication with hallucinations. It has been given much glamour by its use amongst the pop stars, and it has been said many songs have been created under its influence. Just as some of the poets of the 18th and 19th Centuries worked under the influence of Opium or Veronal. In the East it is widely used as an intoxicant. There is a descriptive name for the plant which is evocative and would make an magnificent advertisement. Imagine a hoarding on a motorway with a picture of a leaf against a mysterious background with the caption 'Leaf of Delusion'. The drug barons are all-powerful and the poor people from the third world struggle to survive and sometimes it is through the growing of these illegal crops that they manage. I heard recently that there are plans to ruin these crops by introducing a factor which would cause decomposition. How is it possible to condone this practice in a book which is devoted to the wonders of plant-life? We can condemn even our favourite tipples. It is a tragedy that the addicts have taken away one source of our dreams.

Hemp is potent. It is said that 'it is dangerous to sleep in a field of hemp owing to the aroma of the plants.' There is a distinctive smell about all the materials made from hemp. Sometimes it is the smell in a warehouse where it mingles with the smells of canvas and paraffin.

Without ever having tried a 'joint' I have heard enough about the drug to know how arguments are used to make the drug available to patients who suffer severe pain and in some cases of terminal illnesses. It is a further tragedy that they are denied this one source of solace.

FAVOURITES OF THE PHYSCIANS OF MYDDFAI

The plan to which were part of the Druids 'Seven Sacred Herbs' and plants which have retained some importance in our present medical world.

The Eleven Herbs of the Physicians of Myddfai

Wild sage . . . Good for the brain. Will draw out pain.
The Nettle . . . Full of vitamins and iron and contains essential minerals. Compare to Spinach.
Betony . . . An old writer says Apeliusl 'It is good for the man's sould or for his body. I shields him against visions and dream. Power against evil spirits.'
Iris . . . Purge . . . Ipececuana . . . a cough medicine.
Parsely: Red . . . M. Gieves says it is known from Roman and Grecian and ancient times. Many legends. Many beneficial medicinal properties.
Fennel . . . Rheumatism. Strokes and combined with Lily of the Valley, restorative for people recovering from strokes.
Rosemary.

Blessed Thistle.
Cleavers . . . Goose Grass . . . Sweethearts.
Mistletoe.
Oak . . . The scared tree of the Druids.
Vervain . . . Also endowed with magical powers. There is much written on this subject, i.e. a ring around serpents made of Vervain and they will fight each other. Highly regarded by many nationalities, cultivated in Monasteries. Drives away devils and despair. Vettonica . . . Celtic word 'bew'. Romans sprinkled it on the altars of Jupiter and it was employed in rites of love and as mentioned, a sacred plant of the Druids. Latter-day magicians wear a crown of vervain as protection during the evocation of demons. For centuries vervain has led the botanical field in the treatment of nervous disorders, epilepsy and asthma. It also fortifies the liver, heart and spleen, relieves mental strain and helps cure infectious diseases (a wineglassful of a standard infusion, made from the flowers, leaves and diced stalk, should be taken on rising). The infusion may be used as a gargle or mouth-wash for sore throats and gums or as an eye lotion of considerable merit. Albertus Magnus calls this her 'pisterion' and recommends it for curing inflammation and diseases of the skin. It is an efficient vermifuge.

In a book by David Conway, *The Magic of Herbs*, there is a list of the seven sacred herbs of the Druids. All must have grown in the area. The list is as follows: Mistletoe, this is chief of the sacred flowers connected with Druidism. In his book it is referred to as the 'Golden Bough'. When cut great ceremony was used. The Druids went forth to gather it and were clad in their white robes, they used a golden knife for the purpose and it was cut at a particular age of the moon. The time to gather it however, seemed to be as a direction received in a vision or a dream. If by chance it fell to the ground some misfortune might come to the country.

For me I know it is part of the growth of Mistletoe on the oak tree, which probably meant much in that ancient society. The fact that it grows freely in Brittany, another centre of Druids, is significant, but also it is a favourite food of the Missel Thrush which makes me think well of it. Sheep like it also and when food is scarce in winter, they eat it with relish. So it is said.

Vervain which acts with Valerian and is relaxing and induces sleep. If a decoction of this mixture is made and a pinch of henbane is added it is a stronger narcotic. Vervain is considered effective against evil spirits and a crown of the plant was worn by Druids in their rituals. Other plants in this category is the Primrose, probably the Primrose family is considered and of all these mulled Cowslip wine has more appeal. There is Red Clover, another sleeping mixture, especially with a pillow stuffed with hops; Pulsatilla (Iris with its constituent, Ipecuhana, used more recently in cough mixtures) and Wolf's Bane, (Aconitum Vulparia) regarding this last it seems significant there there is little reference it in all my herbal books. I think this is because it has poisonous properties and to play down its existence is important. I found my note in an ordinary text book on wild flowers. When I was young I thought if I ate the seeds of a fern I would become invisible. It is not so.

My own list is:

Willow . . . aspirin.
Rosemary . . . highly regarded by many nationalities. It is cultivated in Monasteries as it is in our own gardens. It is said to drive away despair. I know it is a valuable culinary herb and an attractive shrub in the garden.
Foxglove . . . Digitalis . . . Important drug used for regulating the heart beat.
Male Fern . . . Antithemetic.
Hawthorn . . . Blood Pressure.
Carrageen . . . Lungs.
Cabbage . . . Poultice. Cooling and for heat.
Poppy . . . Opium.
Marigold . . . Kills germs.
Penny Royal . . . Aids abortion.
Cannabis . . . Mildly hallucinates.
Sphagnum Moss . . . Absorbent.
Comfrey . . . Healing – Knitbone is a good name for it.

If, in this chapter, there will be some repetition, I hope a reader will forgive me. I have found myself confounded by the knowledge that has existed for thousands of years in all parts of the globe. It is strange to find that in different parts of the world the same secrets are discovered. There are results of other people who have been interested, their successes and, as in the case of a Botanist who admired our common Gorse plant and found he could not grow it in his own country. Apparently it is found everywhere except Antartica. Sphagnum Moss was universally respected for its properties of absorption. Comments re its use have been recorded by the Romans and in the seconds from Finland and Scotland.

So, as usual, beginning at the beginning, I must state one plant which must be the one I consider has been most important to me. What else could it be than the Tea Plant. A cup of tea, freshly made when reaching home after a gruelling 'shopping'. Tea in the canteen drunk by miners after reaching the surface after dealing with a disaster. It need not be a major disaster, underground. A cup of tea on the table as friends celebrate or sympathise over someone's sorrow or joy. A cup of tea and an aspirin when a cold or a headache is affecting one.

I could add to the important plants, hops. According to the Myddfai Physicians, there is a sleeping mixture consisting of Red Clover Heads, Lettuce and Hops. I was told a long while ago that a lettuce sandwich before bed time would help one to sleep. It seemed such a simple solution I ignored it. In the context of the above recipe which is in the form of a standard infusion, a cupful before retiring is recommended.

Meadowsweet

There must be a special place for this plant. All through the pages of books used during my searching for secrets grown from Welsh soil, one name keeps occurring. Meadowsweet and a name utterly deserved . . . 'The Queen of The Meadows'.

It was the first recipe given by a friend when she knew that I was writing this book. She was used to the ways of flowers and herbs because of her own particular era . . . in the sixties, younger than myself but born before the years when health shops and a general interest in aromatherapy and natural cures and a commercialization of most of the useful herbs. The recipe was for a drink, it included Meadowsweet.

She described it as a simple, refreshing summer drink.

9 Nettle tops
7 Dandelion leaves
5 Leaves of Meadowsweet
4 Blackcurrant tops
1 stick Rhubarb
Plus sugar and yeast.

For a gallon. Pour on the water when it has boiled and allow the mixture of herbs to infuse. When tepid, float a piece of toast with ½ oz yeast on it, cover and leave it for 3 days. Strain and bottle and drink quickly before 10 days. It would make an excellent extra for a barbecue.

At first I took Meadowsweet for granted, it was only a common flower found in the hedgerows and credited as many others were with many virtues.

Before I continue, while the experience is fresh in my mind I shall relate my first real look at this plant.

I had read so much of it that I could visualise it. I knew it was fragrant, it had a delicate feathery appearance and that it flowered in July where the ground was damp, on the edges of natural meadows. I realised several plants were similar yet I had read so many descriptions that I was certain when I came across this flower I should know it. From my bedroom window I could see along the hedge patches of a lacy, creamy plant. Somehow I was certain this was it and I determined to walk across the soaking field to see for myself. We had a lot of rain and the puddles were deep; I did not have on sensible shoes for it was July, however with my stick and by careful steps from one clump of grass to another I reached the patch. The flowers were just as they had been described and so were the leaves, I looked under one leaf and there was an entirely different shade of green which made me certain . . . and the scent. No wonder all those old houses were strewn with this fragrant plant, leaves and flowers with an individual scent of their own . . . no wonder the Druids regarded this as sacred along with their Vervain and Valerian; no wonder these leaves or petals floating in a drink would make that drink more delicious. I quote from a book, *Common Plants as Natural Remedies* by Cynthia Wickham this information, that this plant was a favourite of Good Queen Bess. Gerard said of it: 'The leaves and flowers of Meadowsweet farre excelle all other strewing herbs for to decke up houses, to strawe in chambers, halls and banqueting houses, for the smell thereof makes the heart merrie and joyful and delighteth the senses.' In Chaucer's time, flowers were boiled in wine and used for ague and to cheer the heart, and the distilled flower water was used as an eye lotion. It is aromatic, astringent, diuretic and a sub-tonic. And as I have mentioned, with vervain and watermint it was one of the three herbs held most sacred by the druids. Of all plants which have been exciting to hold and to smell also to see I think this must one of the foremost. I think the walk across the field to find it made it so.

The mention of it being a sub-tonic must relate to the content of Salicylic acid, in fact the official name for this plant family is Spiraea from which the word Aspirin comes.

This year 1998 is the year I saw Meadowsweet growing in swathes and in the hedges around my fields with sufficient strength to make me notice it. It grows in such places and thrives where the ground is damp and this particular Summer has been very wet. At the moment I am rejoicing because we have had our hay cut and stored and the work was carried out in a fever of energy in case the few dry days would pass. As I walked with unimaginable pleasure across the field when the hay was being turned and turned until each pile was plumped up and I could run my hands through the dried grass and hear a magical rustle, I noticed in the hedges the Meadowsweet was beginning to die off. It occurred to me that there were many plants making a comeback. I think a this might be because for many years we have stopped using fertilizers. Even the farmers discussed this and have now decided that the hay was much more fragrant and less strong without their use.

One plant, which has similar properties and looks almost the same, is Yarrow. This is common all over Europe and is the plant which was recommended to Achilles to dress his wound by Aphrodite after the siege of Troy . . . to ease the pain. Milfoil is another name for this plant and in the Orkney Isles it is used as a tea drunk to dispel melancholy.

This herb does not deserve to be as it is said, dedicated to the devil for it has many uses, not the least is, if it is kept under a sleeper at night it will give that person a glimpse of a future wife or husband. It was used for divination in spells and dried yarrow stems are still used today when consulting the *I Ching*, the Chinese book of changes. It was carried by soldiers when they were engaged in battles because it was useful to stop bleeding. In the old days it was called 'Poor man's snuff' and Culpepper, who strangely, did not mention Meadowsweet, recommends it to be sniffed up the nose to promote sneezing and because of this it is supposed to relieve headaches.

At times the same herb is useful in different spheres. I have been confounded by the knowledge which has existed for thousands of years in all parts of the Globe. An example is a snippet of knowledge . . . a Botanist admired our common Gorse plant and found he could not grow it in his own country, it is found everywhere except Antarctica. Sphagnum Moss was known by the Romans and in Finland, useful in the highlands of Scotland and in hospitals in the Thirties.

If this says anything it is to ask why is this technological generation we have a right to feel superior? Even in this book which is the study of a small area of Wales it proves how far back the area was farmed and I suppose, at times exploited. Perhaps that is why I felt a thrill when I held that stalk of Meadowsweet and considered how important that plant was to the Druids apart from all those generations of people in our past.

One note here re Prickly Lettuce. This is a form of lettuce which is poisonous. The innocuous name must not make people confuse it with ordinary garden lettuce. It has certain properties. An American took a tea made from the leaves to stimulate the flow of mill. This is yet another example of never taking medicine, even if it sounds innocent, without taking wise advice.

LINSEED

It was the plant to which the plague of hail proved to be disastrous. In Genesis XII, v.42, Joseph was arrayed in this product as was also the Jewish High Priests and the curtains in the Tabernacle. It formed the clothing of the Saviour in the tomb where he was laid by Joseph of Arimathea. Even now it is one fabric which is cool and classical and has the feel of elegance which makes it hard to remember it is the product of a plant. This plant was cultivated back into the remotest periods of history and I have a linen blouse I bought last year from the High Street. The wearing of fine linen is a timeless phrase.

Pliny writes 'What department is there to be found in active life in which Flax is not employed. It was familiar in the countries of Egypt, Italy Galerius and Babillus, from Alexander to the Straits of Cicily. Do not forget the trading vessels from Phoenicia that sailed along the rivers in Cornwall.

Searching through the pages of the many books about herbs I have learnt much and have been amazed constantly as I realise that most of the knowledge has been available for hundred or even thousands of years. So much has been forgotten. So many snippets of information, for example even about that Mares' Tail, the oldest of our plants, the one which is the bane of a gardeners' life. I did not know that a bunch of this was used to scour pans. Yet if one considers it is harsh and could be used for that purpose.

I shall remember Sorrel or Sower Sabs: Dandelions or 'Pee the Bed'; Foxglove and Digitalis: Poppy and Opium: Aspirin from Willow or Meadowsweet. All useful and medicinal and as important to us as Cocaine which is found in the Brazilian forests.

And always the swaying branches of the Elderflower.

Any person who reads this work, which makes no claim to be an authority on the detailed knowledge of herbs only to record a few strange basics or proven factors in natural lore, will appreciate that I write from the stand-point of my span of a simple life spent close to Nature.

I make no pretenses. I am, without affectation sometimes associated with the comment, a free spirit. Among my many faults the worst is the craving to possess. So much I gain and I throw very little away. In later years there is a softening in this approach and I part with possessions if I feel they will be more useful elsewhere.

There is the opposite side of the coin. I need to possess all things natural. My plants, weeds, spectacular and those lost in the hedgerow, even the devious little purple Deadly Nightshade; flowers which have been allowed to spread extravagantly; birds, the chaffinch with an injured leg, a leg which was partly pulled out but healed and this bird has weathered a third winter since, an example of ornithological courage; an old crow who perches on a clothes line pole. There are the scraps of paper, secret notes on plants, maps, grid references. With imperial impudence I consider the natural world is mine and that includes its secrets.

Amongst my favourites I have included the plants which have produced substances which are used in orthodox medicine. There are others which might have deserved inclusion but these are recognised, e.g. salicylic acid or aspirin is an example to be found in the Willow and Meadowsweet. Aspirin is a household name, it is advocated on a regular basis in some cardiac conditions and rheumatic conditions. I am sure the financial firms have considered herbal properties in plants which might avoid some side effects of an aspirin tablet. Wintergreen is an obvious example of usefulness in liniments.

If there is one plant in my opinion, lowly as that is, that this plant is the professional. I will state with assurance, it is the Foxglove which gives Digitalin. It even looks the part. It stands out with such confidence amongst its contemporaries on grassy banks and in the hedgerow. It holds its own against those who would effect a 'take-over'. The plant grown naturally produces seeds of a better quality than those grown on a commercial basis. It defies the current diminishing of the species. Its public relations cannot be questioned. Its strength and energy proves its obvious power, a leader's essential quality, its regal colour and profuse flowering ability could never be questioned. Interest in the plant over the years has been shown by the affectionate names it has been given, Ladies' Glove. Folksglove (which some say was the origin of the real name) Fairies' Glove, Folksglove was a name because the plant was supposed to grow in one of those dells where the fairies were living and of course fairies were the good folk. Amongst the many different names for the plant, most made reference in some way to the shape of the flower, a glove or a bell, there is only one foreign translation from the Norwegian which has any reference to the fox . . . once again all this information is contained in Mrs Grieve's *A Modern Herbal*. The name matches the plant which is instantly recognisable and like Cadburys or Shredded Wheat is recognisable wherever it grows.

It has been used in the past, most of the Herbalists mention it,

Culpepper writes of its gentle and cleansing nature and that the juice will promote healing on old sores, but perhaps their knowledge at the time was insufficient to appreciate the essential medicinal value which was contained in it, Digitalis Purpurea. The specialists know exactly when to gather the fresh leaves for this important contribution to medicine.

Although it is not mentioned in my list the following plant is included in many ancient catalogues.

It seems to have its own personality, almost as strong in such a different manner. I would like to say a word for Fumitory. This is the opposite of Foxglove . . . instead of power there is mysticism. It has even been suspected of appearing out of the ground, born, as the ancients say, out of the vapours of the earth. I has a magical aura. It is smoky and ethereal and fascinating. It does possess some qualities. Its juice is employed to clear the eyesight, 'brings tears to the eyes, just like smoke.' It is employed internally and externally . . . to cleanse the liver and eliminate toxins from the body and is accompanied with the warning that to take an infusion or as a mild decoction (20-80 grams to a litre of water) one cupful three times a day as an aperient, tonic depurative changes and the treatment proceeds to be sedative and hypnotic. It is so mysterious. It will also cleanse the skin . . . peasant girls used to boil it in milk to remove a summer tan from their faces. With a sigh I state, those peasant girls had the milk and the sun to tan their complexions.

I suppose that the readers of this book will realise that I have written at random about plants and places where they grow because I have found these details interesting. I write from a standpoint of a simple life spent close to nature, in my youth to a small town close to the country and the sea and in most of my later years in rural Wales. Perhaps in my own way and I say this without any self disillusionment, I am a free spirit yet that freedom has been tempered by years of training in orthodox medicines. Therefore, the plants which fascinate are those which have affected medicine in some way, perhaps it is the fact that for so many thousands of years people have known just as much as we have known, forgotten much more and our only advantage is that time has given us the power to understand how to apply that knowledge.

Bibliography

PLINY	
CULPEPPER	
MRS. M. GRIEVES	*A Modern Herbal.*
CYNTHIA WICKHAM	*Common Plants as Natural Remedies.*
JOHN LUST	*The Herb Book.*
JEAN PALAISEUL	*Grandmother's Secrets.*
NATIONAL FEDERATION OF WOMEN'S INSTITUTES	*Cornish Recipes.*
DAVID CONWAY	*The Magic of Herbs.*
NORA CHADWICK	*The Celts.*
MR. NOEL GIBBARD	Ms. from Llanelli Library.
DR. DEREK PRYCE	*Herbal Remedies of the Physicians of Myddfai.*
MANACCON W.I.	
ROGER BANKS	*A Wild Garden.*
MUNTING	*The True British Herbs of the Ancients.*
SUSAN CAMPBELL	*Garden dose.*
JOHN AND ROSEMARY HEMPHILL	*Herbs and Spices.*